SPECTRUM SERIES
PHONICS

Published 1997 McGraw-Hill Learning Materials

TABLE OF CONTENTS

STRUCTURAL ANALYSIS

VOCABULARY

DICTIONARY SKILLS

INSTRUCTIONAL CONSULTANT
Mary Lou Maples, Ed.D.
Chairman of Department of Education
Huntingdon College
Montgomery, Alabama

EDITORIAL AND PRODUCTION STAFF
Series Editor: Joyce R. Rhymer; *Project Editor:* Connie Johnson Long;
Production Editor: Carole R. Hill; *Senior Designer:* Patrick J. McCarthy;
Associate Designer: Terry D. Anderson; *Project Artist:* Gilda Braxton Edwards;
Artist: Shirley J. Beltz; *Illustrator:* Susan Lexa

6 7 8 9 10 POH 03 02 01

Organized for successful learning!

The SPECTRUM PHONICS SERIES builds the right skills for reading.

The program combines four important skill strands — phonics, structural analysis, vocabulary, and dictionary skills — so your students build the skills they need to become better readers.

Four types of lesson pages offer thorough, clearly focused, systematic skills practice. That means you can focus on just the skills that need work — for the whole class, a small group, or for individualized instruction.

The SPECTRUM PHONICS SERIES is easy for students to use independently.

Although phonics may be an important part of a reading program, sometimes there just isn't enough time to do it all. That's why PHONICS offers uncomplicated lessons your children can succeed with on their own.

Colorful borders capture interest, highlight essential information, and help organize lesson structure. And your children get off to a good start with concise explanations and clear directions . . . followed by sample answers that show them exactly what to do.

In addition, vocabulary has been carefully controlled so your children work with familiar words. Key pictures and key words are used consistently throughout the series to represent specific sounds. And a sound-symbol chart at the back of the text helps your students quickly recall sound-symbol relationships.

INSTRUCTION PAGE . . . The skill being covered is noted at the bottom of each student page for easy reference.

REINFORCEMENT PAGE . . .
Comprehension exercises that use context as well as phonics skills to help build the connection from decoding to comprehension.

Turn page for more information.

3

Easy to manage

REVIEW PAGES . . . Frequent reviews emphasize skills application.

ASSESSMENT PAGES . . . Assessment pages give you helpful feedback on how your students are doing.

ANSWER KEY . . . Gives you the help you need when you need it — including student pages with answers for quick, easy reference.

PROGRESS CHECK — Consonant Pairs

Name _____

Read each set of sentences and its list of words. Write the word from the list that makes sense in each sentence.

1. My family likes to _watch_ parades.
2. We always go early so that we can sit on a _____
3. The last parade we saw had _____ marching bands.
4. I clapped as I saw each one _____ by.
5. When I knew the tunes, I would _____ along.
6. I was surprised to see a float being pulled by an _____

march
laugh
thumb
watch
elephant
bench
sing
thirty
catch

REVIEW — Consonant Pairs

Name _____

Read each clue. Write **sh, ch, wh, ng,** or **gh** to complete the word that matches the clue.

1. a food made from milk — _ch_ eese
2. something you blow into that makes a high noise — _____istle
3. a tool used for digging — _____ovel
4. two pieces of bread with meat between them — sandwi_____
5. a playground toy you can sit on — swi_____
6. hard to cut — tou_____
7. something you make when you jump into water — spla_____

shelf
both
wish
whisper
three
white
shake
change
think

Read each clue. Write **th, ph, thr,** or **tch** to complete the word that matches the clue.

1. something that can feel sore when you have a cold — _thr_ oat
2. a number greater than two — _____ee
3. a picture taken with a camera — _____oto
4. a part of your hand — _____umb
5. a piece of cloth that covers a hole in a piece of clothing — pa_____
6. something that is used to make clothes — clo_____
7. something used to light a candle — ma_____

Review of words containing initial and final consonant digraphs

85

Prefixes

Teaching Suggestion 8, Page T-14   Extending Activity 25, Page T-22

Name _____

Words to use: unlock, dislike, repaint, unload, discolor, repaid, overcrowd, mistreat, misspell, overflow, unwrap, distrust, preschool, unpack, rewrap, pregame, misprint

Read each sentence and the word beside it. Add **un-, pre-,** or **over-** to the word to complete each sentence. Write the new word in the blank. The word you form must make sense in the sentence.

1. The _unfair_ rules were changed. — fair
2. I _prepaid_ the cost at the time I ordered. — paid
3. If you don't wake her, she will _oversleep_. — sleep
4. My dog _overeats_ when there is too much food in the dish. — eats
5. Because I lost the game, I felt _unlucky_. — lucky
6. Scott talks about his _preschool_ class. — school

Read each sentence and the word beside it. Add **dis-, re-,** or **mis-** to the word to complete each sentence. Write the new word in the blank. The word you form must make sense in the sentence.

1. If you _disagree_ with me, let me know. — agree
2. Grandma will _retell_ many of her stories. — tell
3. I often _misjudge_ the time when I get busy. — judge
4. I will _reheat_ the chicken soup for lunch. — heat
5. We saw the rabbit _disappear_ from sight into the red hat. — appear
6. If you _misread_ the sign, you will get lost. — read

Beginning Sounds

Name _____

Read the words and name the pictures. Circle the word that names each picture.

goat	van	came
note	man	tame
vote	can	game
(coat)	tan	name

fan	face	jaw
can	case	saw
pan	vase	raw
van	lace	law

Read the sentences. Complete the unfinished word in each sentence by writing the beginning consonant. The word you form must make sense in the sentence.

1. Please _j_oin us when we go camping next weekend.

2. You can ____ead the map to see where we are going.

3. We will begin our trip in the ____orning.

4. It will not take us long to set up the ____ents when we get to the park.

5. When we get to the lake, we will fly ____ites.

6. We may be able to go ____ike riding.

7. When it is dark, we will build a ____ire.

8. I will teach you how to sing a new ____ong.

9. Will you say "____es" and come with us?

Beginning Sounds

Name _____

Look at the pictures. Write the letter or letters that stand for the beginning sound of each picture name.

_f_ork

____ail

____ink

____ipper

_____een

____ose

Read each sentence and the word beside it. In each line, change the first letter of the word in dark print to form a new word that will make sense in the sentence. Write the word in the blank.

1. I went to a pet show at the school last ___*night*___.   **might**

2. I have never seen so many cats and _____.   **hogs**

3. One boy had a _____ bird.   **walking**

4. A small boy brought a basket that held three _____.   **mittens**

5. Another girl had a tank filled with _____.   **wish**

6. I even saw a girl showing a pet _____.   **big**

7. The _____ pets were given prizes.   **west**

8. Picking the winners must have been a hard _____.   **rob**

Ending Sounds

Name _____

Read the words and name the pictures. Circle the word that names each picture.

bib	tab	can
bid	tag	cap
big	tan	car
bit	tap	cat

bud	mat	hat
bus	map	had
bun	mad	ham
bug	man	has

Read the sentences. Complete the unfinished word in each sentence by writing the ending consonant. The word you form must make sense in the sentence.

1. Let me tell you what I di_d_ last week.

2. I too____ my first airplane ride over the city.

3. My ride was one afternoon after schoo____.

4. A friend of my da____ flew the small plane.

5. From the air I could see the tall buildings on my stree____.

6. Each car and bu____ that I saw looked like a little toy.

7. I could see the playground and the roo____ of our school.

8. Seeing the city from the air was a lot of fu____.

Symbol-sound association of words containing final consonants; Words containing final consonants in context

Ending Sounds

Name _____

Name the pictures. Write the letter that stands for the ending sound of each picture name.

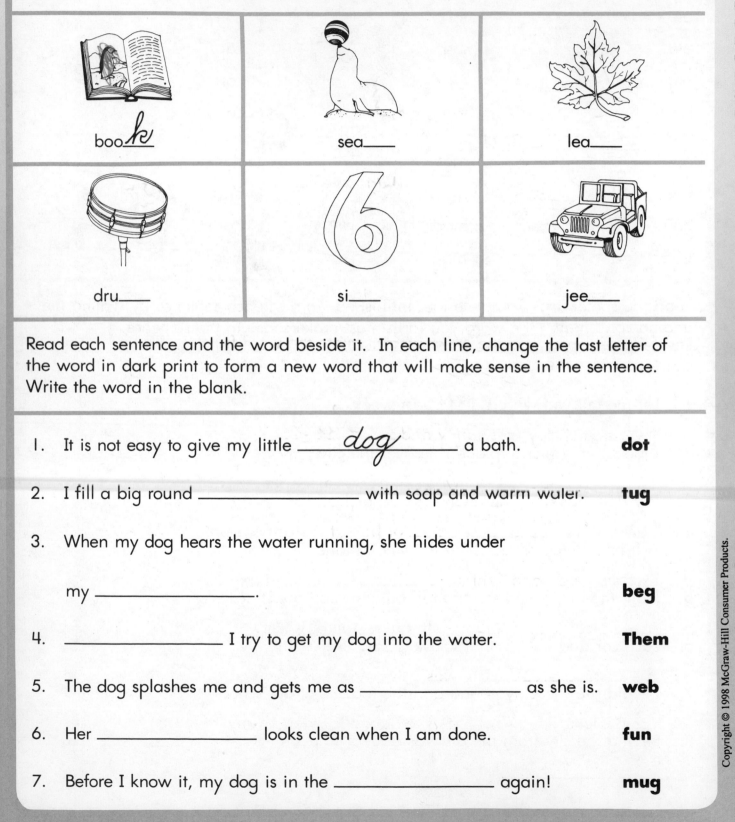

boo_k_

sea____

lea____

dru____

si____

jee____

Read each sentence and the word beside it. In each line, change the last letter of the word in dark print to form a new word that will make sense in the sentence. Write the word in the blank.

1. It is not easy to give my little ___*dog*___ a bath.   **dot**

2. I fill a big round _____ with soap and warm water.   **tug**

3. When my dog hears the water running, she hides under

    my _____.   **beg**

4. _____ I try to get my dog into the water.   **Them**

5. The dog splashes me and gets me as _____ as she is. **web**

6. Her _____ looks clean when I am done.   **fun**

7. Before I know it, my dog is in the _____ again!   **mug**

Sound-symbol association of final consonants; Words containing final consonants in context

Beginning and Ending Sounds

Name _____

Name the pictures. Write the letters that stand for the consonant sounds of each picture name.

_S_eve_n_

___ a ___

___ o o ___

___ o o ___

___ ige ___

___ e a ___

Read the sentences and the list of words. Write the word from the list that makes sense in each sentence.

1. The summer day was sunny and ___ *hot* ___.

2. My _____ was to catch as many fish as I could.

3. I bought a _____ of bait at the corner store.

4. I took my bait and fishing _____ to the lake.

5. I _____ my fish into a pail of water.

6. The _____ was going down as I walked to my tent.

7. After a long day of fishing, it felt good to sleep on my

   _____.

not

sun

lot

put

job

rod

cot

hot

get

Assessment of sound-symbol association of initial and final consonants; Words containing initial and final consonants in context

Short Vowels

Name _____

Read the words and name the pictures. Circle the word that names each picture.

tan (ten) tip top	top tab tip tap	tug tin tag tan
ran rug run rag	bed bag big bug	clap clam clock click
pen pat pin pan	step stop ship shop	not nest net nut
pig pen pin peg	fans fist fish fast	cap cub cab cup

Symbol-sound association of short-vowel words

Short Vowels

Name _____

Name the pictures. Write the letter that stands for the vowel sound of each picture name.

bl__ck

l___mp

br___sh

ch___mney

l___ck

w___ll

d___ck

t___nt

br___ck

h___t

p___nny

f___x

Sound-symbol association of short vowels

Short Vowels

Name _____

Read the words and name the pictures. Circle the word that names each picture.

| (tag) tip top tug | | pen pit pot pan | | hot hat hill hem | |
| men map mop man | | luck lick lock lack | | lad leg lid log | |

Read the sentences. In the blanks below each sentence, write the words from the sentence that have a short-vowel sound. Do not write the words **a** or **the.**

1. These new red pants feel baggy.

    red   _pants_   _baggy_

2. My old hat is bright yellow.

    _____   _____   _____

3. My green socks have big stripes.

    _____   _____

4. I feel like a funny circus clown.

    _____   _____

Symbol-sound association of short-vowel words; Identifying short-vowel words in context

Short Vowels

Name _____

Read each set of sentences and its list of words. Write the word from the list that makes sense in each sentence.

1. Many of my school friends started a _____*club*_____.

2. We like to go hiking and _____ at nearby places.

3. Tomorrow we _____ to go on a hike through the woods.

4. You can meet _____ early in the morning.

5. You will get hungry, so remember to bring a _____.

6. If you need a backpack, I can _____ you one.

7. My father _____ take us to the park.

club
us
luck
camping
can
plan
stamp
lend
lunch

8. Jack's mom will _____ us home.

9. I hope we have a _____ day.

10. We'll talk about the hike the _____ time we meet.

11. Carlos _____ show us his pictures.

12. Sally might bring the _____ and leaves she finds.

13. Kim will _____ us about other parks.

14. We may want to talk about taking a camping _____.

15. When the morning is over, we can eat a _____.

jump
will
next
bring
rocks
snack
pick
sunny
tell
trip

Short-vowel words in context

Short Vowels

Name _____

Read the sentences. Complete the unfinished word in each sentence by writing the missing vowel. The word you form must make sense in the sentence.

1. I visited the farm animals l*a*st week.

2. I w___nt inside the big red barn with my friend Maria.

3. There I saw a large p___g sleeping in the corner of a pen.

4. Many young pigs ran around in another large p___n.

5. I could tell they liked running in the m___d.

6. It was fun to sp___nd time looking at the pigs.

7. Outside I saw a b___g horse.

8. My friend showed me how it could tr___t around the barn.

9. She also showed me how to br___sh the horse's coat.

10. The horse l___t me pet its nose.

11. Its nose felt warm and s___ft.

12. Now I w___sh I had a horse of my own.

13. I can't have one in my c___ty apartment.

14. So, I'll go b___ck to visit the farm again.

Assessment of short-vowel words in context

Long Vowels

Name _____

Read the words and look at the pictures. Circle the word that tells about each picture.

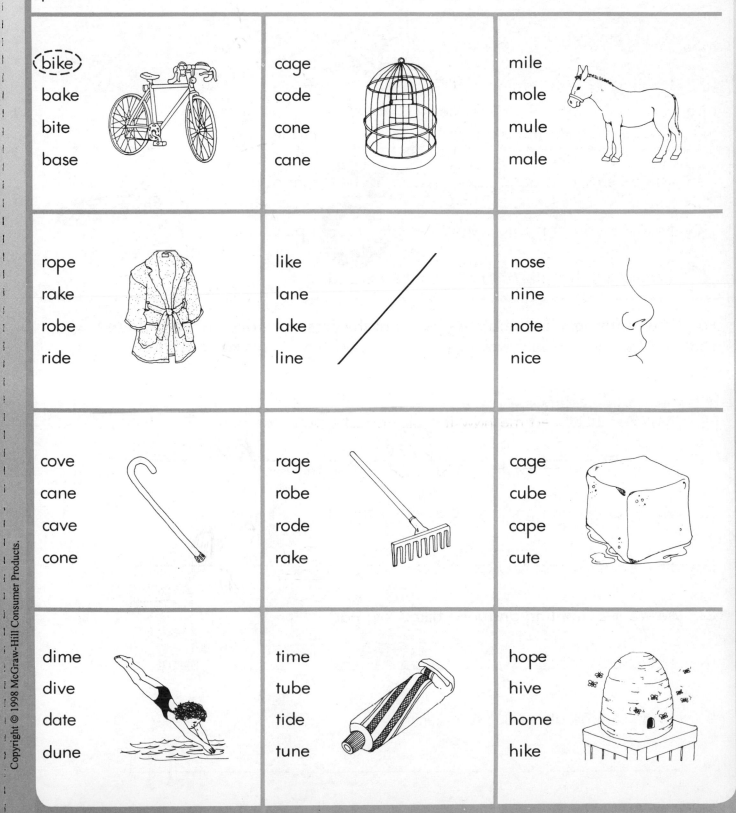

(bike)	cage	mile
bake	code	mole
bite	cone	mule
base	cane	male
rope	like	nose
rake	lane	nine
robe	lake	note
ride	line	nice
cove	rage	cage
cane	robe	cube
cave	rode	cape
cone	rake	cute
dime	time	hope
dive	tube	hive
date	tide	home
dune	tune	hike

Symbol-sound association of long-vowel words

Long Vowels

Name _____

Read the words and look at the pictures. Circle the word that tells about each picture.

rise rope (rose) ripe	skate slide snake slope	home hide hive hose
time tape take tide	fine fake five face	time tile tube tune

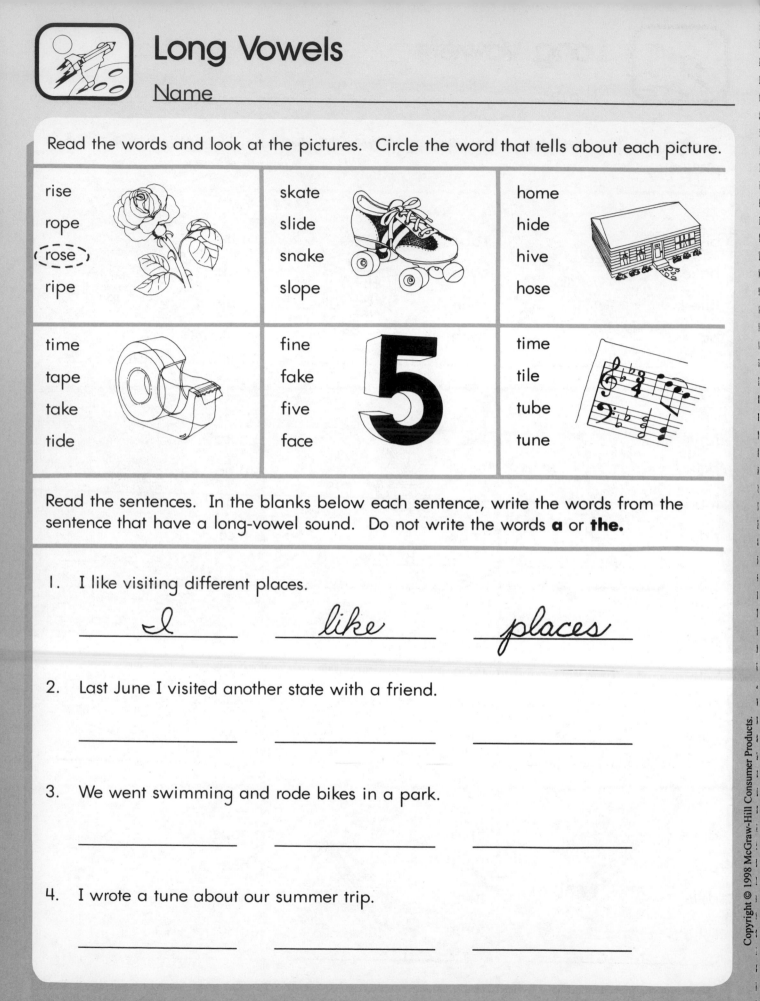

Read the sentences. In the blanks below each sentence, write the words from the sentence that have a long-vowel sound. Do not write the words **a** or **the.**

1. I like visiting different places.

   _____I_____   _____like_____   _____places_____

2. Last June I visited another state with a friend.

   _____   _____   _____

3. We went swimming and rode bikes in a park.

   _____   _____   _____

4. I wrote a tune about our summer trip.

   _____   _____   _____

Symbol-sound association of long-vowel words; Identifying long-vowel words in context

Long Vowels

Name _____

Look at the pictures. Write the letter or letters that stand for the vowel sound in each picture name.

r _a_ k _e_   r __ p __   g __ m __

c __ b __   b __ k __   st __ v __

n __ n __   l __ c __   fl __ t __

r __ c __   h __ v __   b __ n __

Sound-symbol association of long-vowel words

17

Long Vowels

Name _____

Read the sentences. Complete the unfinished word in each sentence by writing the missing vowel. The word you form must make sense in the sentence.

1. It was l_a_te one night when I heard the noise.

2. I had been sleeping, and the noise w___ke me.

3. I didn't have a clock, so I'm not sure what t___me it was.

4. The wh___te light of the moon lit my bedroom.

5. I h___te to say that I was feeling afraid.

6. Again I heard the s___me sound.

7. I must have looked p___le as I sat up in bed.

8. I felt myself starting to sh___ke.

9. I remember telling myself to be br___ve.

10. I got out of bed and put on a warm r___be.

11. I called my cat's n___me.

12. A sound c___me from the toy box in a corner of my room.

13. Guess who had found a new place to h___de?

14. I felt myself begin to sm___le.

15. The cat looked c___te as she jumped out of the toy box when I opened it.

Long-vowel words in context

OLD and IND

Name _____

The letter **o** followed by **ld** usually stands for the long-**o** sound. The letter **i** followed by **nd** usually stands for the long-**i** sound.

c**old**
k**ind**

Read each sentence and words beside it. Write the word that makes sense in each sentence.

1. Did you get _cold_ while you were waiting for the bus?	cone cold cot
2. When I got a new bike, I _____ my old one.	sold soak sock
3. Would you _____ going shopping with me?	mix mine mind
4. Little children like to _____ our puppy.	hold home hoe
5. Please keep your reading papers in this _____.	colder folder older
6. Were you able to _____ the button you lost?	find fin fine
7. What _____ of eggs shall I cook today?	kind king kite
8. Linc said to my teacher, "I am feeling _____."	find fin fine
9. Were you at home when Luis _____ you the news?	fold told cold

Words containing *old* and *ind* in context

OLD and *IND*

Name _____

Read the sentences and the list of words. Write the word from the list that makes sense in each sentence.

1. It was ___*kind*___ of you to walk my dog.

2. The shop on the corner _____ balloons and kites.

3. The workers will _____ the meat while you wait.

4. I'm having trouble _____ my math paper.

5. Do you know where we can buy a candle _____ to set on our new table?

6. Visiting Denny was the _____ thing you could do for him.

7. After we do the wash, we must _____ the clothes.

8. His ride through the snowstorm showed that the prince was

    _____.

9. Would you _____ if I bring my brother and sister with me?

10. The park worker _____ us about the animals that live in the woods.

11. Seeing-eye dogs are used to lead _____ persons.

12. I keep all of my school papers in a large _____.

13. Which of the five bicycles is the _____?

fold

finding

told

blind

grind

holder

oldest

kind

bold

sold

mind

kindest

folder

Words containing *old* and *ind* in context

Long Vowels

Name _____

Read each set of sentences and its list of words. Write the word from the list that makes sense in each sentence.

1. Last spring I ___*wrote*___ a letter to my aunt.

2. I wanted to visit her _____ for a week.

3. She said it would be _____ for me to visit.

4. One night I flew there in a huge _____.

5. We were lucky that we didn't have one _____ day.

6. We spent a lot of time _____.

7. I wanted to _____ some rocks to take to school.

8. I found many _____ cones, too.

wrote

cold

nice

flute

outside

home

find

plane

told

pine

---

1. One day I helped my aunt by using a _____ in the garden.

2. For fun, I jumped into a _____ of straw.

3. Each evening, I fed the _____ calf.

4. Before the sun went down, I would _____ the pony.

5. After dinner, my uncle would play a _____ for us on his flute.

6. He showed me how he reads the _____ of each song.

pile

cute

grind

rake

notes

sold

tune

ride

Assessment of long-vowel words in context

21

Short and Long Vowels

Name the pictures. Write the letter or letters that stand for the vowel sound of each picture name.

f __i__ v e   l __ __ k   s __ __ n

b __ __ d   r __ __ p   f __ __ n

r __ __ k   g __ __ ld   d __ __ m

fl __ __ t   p __ __ g   t __ __ p

Sound-symbol association of short- and long-vowel words

Short and Long Vowels

Name _____

Read the sentences. Complete the unfinished word in each sentence by writing the missing vowel or vowels. The word you form must make sense in the sentence.

1. The family garden is in b_a_ck of the house.

2. Every spring, I h__lp my mother plant the seeds.

3. First we use a shovel to d__g up the soil.

4. We use a r__k to make the soil smooth.

5. Then the seeds are planted in n__n straight rows.

6. The summer s__n helps the plants grow.

7. I pick every ripe green bean that I can f__nd.

8. We begin going to the market in J__n.

9. We t__k a lot of the food that grew in our garden.

10. The food is s__ld from the back of our new truck.

11. I put each person's food in a paper b__g.

12. Sometimes I s__t and watch the people.

13. The bright shining sun makes me h__t.

14. It makes me want to j__mp into a lake.

15. That's just what my d__d lets me do after we leave the market.

Short- and long-vowel words in context

Short and Long Vowels

Name _____

Read each sentence and the words beside it. Write the word that makes sense in each sentence.

1. We should ___*stop*___ at Abby's costume shop.		stop step stone
2. She will _____ us try on some clothes.		let led leg
3. You might enjoy looking at the _____.		must masks most
4. You'll also like trying on each hat you _____.		fin find fine
5. I _____ to dress up as a big white bunny.		like lake line
6. Dressing like a football player is _____, too.		fun fan fin
7. My brother looks _____ in an elf costume.		cut cute cube
8. If you want to fool people, wear a curly _____.		wag wig wide
9. Wouldn't you look strange in long _____ hair?		pink pine pin
10. If you want to look like a clown, wear a shiny red _____.		nice nose name

Short- and long-vowel words in context

Short and Long Vowels

Name _____

Read each set of sentences and its list of words. Write the word from the list that makes sense in each sentence.

1. When we ___*camp*___, I like to hike in the nearby woods.

2. I pick up each pine _____ I see.

3. I sometimes find a bird's _____ that is filled with eggs.

4. A small animal sometimes comes out of a _____ in the ground.

5. I carefully watch where I _____.

6. I want the animals to be _____.

7. Someday I will _____ a story about the things I have seen in the woods.

write
camp
step
ship
cone
mind
safe
nest
hole

---

1. My grandfather's house is near the bank of a _____.

2. I feed the _____ when I visit.

3. I like to watch them _____ around.

4. To get sun, they sit on a flat _____.

5. All the ducks march in a _____.

6. They look so _____.

7. I _____ I lived near a pond as Grandfather does.

wish
line
hold
pond
cute
ducks
swim
rock
stamp

Short- and long-vowel words in context

Short and Long Vowels

Name _____

Read each sentence and the words beside it. Write the word that makes sense in each sentence.

1. Randy will be _____*ten*_____ years old on his birthday.

ten
tan
ton

2. We are beginning to _____ a surprise party.

plan
plane
plant

3. Kristy will _____ our friends about the party.

tall
talk
tell

4. Bobby and Sandy can _____ a cake.

back
bake
base

5. Jeff will teach us a new _____ of game.

king
kind
kick

6. Let's make a _____ sign that says, "Happy Birthday."

hug
huge
hum

7. When it's time, Randy's grandmother will _____ him to the store.

sand
send
sent

8. We will _____ behind the chairs in his house.

hid
hide
hive

9. Jill will begin the birthday _____.

tune
tube
tub

10. I _____ Randy will be surprised!

hope
hop
home

Assessment of short- and long-vowel words in context

Hard and Soft C and G

Name _____

Symbol-sound association of hard- and soft-*c* and hard- and soft-*g* words

The letters **c** or **g** followed by **e, i,** or **y** usually stand for their soft sounds, as in **cent** and **page**. The letters **c** or **g** followed by any other letters usually stand for their hard sounds, as in **cat** and **wagon**.

cent
(soft **c**)

pa**ge**
(soft **g**)

Read the words and name the pictures. Draw a line from each word to the picture it names.

city
cube

game
stage

giraffe
garden

card
celery

pig
cage

calf
face

Hard and Soft C and G

Name _____

Read the lists of words. Notice the sound that **c** or **g** stands for in each word. Then write each word under the correct heading.

cent
(soft **c**)

pa**ge**
(soft **g**)

contest	goose	place	dragon	goat
price	cow	stage	cabin	calf
fence	guess	cab	gentle	judge
bridge	center	wig	edge	excited

Hard c as in cat

contest

_____

_____

_____

_____

Soft c as in cent

_____

_____

_____

_____

Hard g as in wagon

_____

_____

_____

_____

Soft g as in page

_____

_____

_____

_____

Symbol-sound association of hard- and soft-c and hard- and soft-g words

Hard and Soft C and G

Name _____

cent
(soft **c**)

pa**ge**
(soft **g**)

Read the sentences. In the blanks below each sentence, write the words from the sentence that have soft **c** or **g.**

1. Gail moved to a city with a well-known bridge.

    city _bridge_

2. The picture on that page shows a gentle giant.

    _____ _____ _____

3. The judge will hear the first case in this place.

    _____ _____

Read the sentences. In the blanks below each sentence, write the words from the sentence that have hard **c** or **g.**

1. Can you get the cat before it runs under the fence?

    Can _get_ _cat_

2. We raced to catch the goat in the garden.

    _____ _____ _____

3. The cow was excited when it got outside the gate.

    _____ _____ _____

Hard and Soft C and G

Name _____

Read the sentences and the words beside them. Write the word that makes sense in each sentence.

1. Please sign this birthday ____*card*____.

2. We can send it to our friend in the _____.

city
cost
card

3. Read the words on the first _____ of this book.

4. They tell you how to play a running _____.

cage
page
game

5. Would you like a _____ of wheat bread?

6. Should I fill your _____ with milk?

cup
cent
slice

7. The park is near the _____ that crosses the stream.

8. Wing likes to look at the flower _____ there.

bridge
car
garden

9. When the play begins, I am standing on the _____.

10. She will sing a very _____ song.

wagon
gentle
stage

11. Did you like the animal shows in the _____?

12. I thought the monkeys were _____.

price
circus
cute

13. Do you like the taste of _____?

14. I can _____ some for you to try.

center
cook
rice

Review of hard- and soft-c and hard- and soft-g words in context

Hard and Soft C and G

Name _____

Read each sentence. Circle the word **hard** or **soft** to tell the kind of sound the **c** or **g** in dark print stands for. Remember: **Cent** and **page** have soft sounds. **Cat** and **wagon** have hard sounds.

		(hard)
1.	Where will the cooking **c**ontest be held?	soft
		hard
2.	There is a bicycle shop in the **c**enter of the town.	soft
		hard
3.	My make-believe story is about an unhappy fro**g**.	soft
		hard
4.	What kind of **g**ame should we play?	soft
		hard
5.	After he ran two miles his fa**c**e was red.	soft
		hard
6.	Will you help me choose a **c**andle?	soft
		hard
7.	Her father bought her a new silver bra**c**elet.	soft
		hard
8.	Lin wore a long black wi**g** at the costume party.	soft
		hard
9.	Do you know the pri**c**e of that football shirt?	soft
		hard
10.	The **g**iraffe has a long neck.	soft
		hard
11.	Stand away from the ed**g**e of the cliff.	soft

Assessment of hard- and soft-c and hard and soft-g words

Two-Letter Blends

Name _____

In some words, one consonant follows another consonant. To say these words, blend the sounds of the two consonants together.

stop   **tw**in
play   **sq**uirrel
green

Read the words and look at the pictures. Circle the word that tells about each picture.

(crib) trip grin drip	clock float block glove	trap snap slap clap
grown brown frown crown	stone smoke spoke slope	dry cry fry pry
flow glow slow snow	black clam flag glass	spot slide stir squirrel
twice twin twine twig	flame plane slate plate	draw tray gray crab

Symbol-sound association of words containing *tw, s, l,* and *r* blends

Two-Letter Blends

Name _____

Read each sentence and the words beside it. Write the word that makes sense in each sentence.

1. I like to roller ___*skate*___ outdoors.

state
skate
slate

2. I _____ at my house and skate to the park.

smart
start
scarf

3. If I think I'm going to fall, I hold onto a _____.

free
tree
glee

4. I am careful not to trip on each _____ of the sidewalk.

crack
track
black

5. The smooth path in the park helps me to _____.

glide
twin
slid

6. My arms _____ as I skate along the path.

sting
swing
skip

7. The soft _____ feels good in my hair.

breeze
freeze
green

8. I sometimes _____ about flying through the air.

great
twenty
dream

9. I meet two people on the path and _____ between them.

sweater
squeeze
speech

10. After skating I am tired, but I feel _____!

great
cream
treat

Words containing *tw, s, l,* and *r* blends in context

Two-Letter Blends

Name _____

Read the sentences. Complete the unfinished word in each sentence by writing the missing blend. Choose from the following blends: **sw, cl, fl, br, fr, sq.** The word you form must make sense in the sentence.

1. Please help me _*cl*_ean my dirty bedroom.

2. I will pick up the clothes from the _____oor.

3. Would you _____eep the floor with this broom?

4. My brother's toy _____uirrel is under the bed.

5. Here is the _____ush that I thought was lost.

6. Now I can walk _____om place to place without tripping over things!

Read the sentences. Complete the unfinished word in each sentence by writing the missing blend. Choose from the following blends: **tw, sc, sn, sp, st, gl, sl.** The word you form must make sense in the sentence.

1. Grandfather will _*sc*_old me if I get up.

2. He said I should try to _____eep.

3. I guess he heard me _____eezing this morning.

4. My _____in sister had a cold before I did.

5. She had to _____end two days in bed last weekend.

6. She told me that Grandfather can also tell a good _____ory any time of day.

7. I am _____ad that Grandfather is here.

Words containing *tw, s, l,* and *r* blends in context

Two-Letter Blends

REVIEW

Name _____

Read each clue. Complete the word beside it to form a word that matches the clue. Choose from the following blends: **tw, sl, sm, st, sw.** You may use a blend more than once.

1. something you need to mail a letter   _st_amp

2. the number before thirteen   _____elve

3. a toy used to ride on snow   _____ed

4. something you can do in a pool or lake   _____im

5. to mix food   _____ir

6. something you do when you are happy   _____ile

Read each clue. Complete the word beside it to form a word that matches the clue. Choose from the following blends: **bl, fl, br, gr, tr, cr, sq.**

1. the color of the sky   _bl_ue

2. a path   _____ail

3. a kind of fruit that grows on a vine   _____ape

4. something that hangs on a pole   _____ag

5. something that can be made into toast   _____ead

6. a shape that has four sides of the same length   _____uare

7. a loud noise   _____ash

Review of words containing *tw, s, l,* and *r* blends

35

Copyright © 1998 McGraw-Hill Consumer Products.

Three-Letter Blends

Name _____

In some words, the letter **s** is followed by two other consonants. To say these words, blend the sound of **s** with the sounds of the consonants that follow.

spring
scream
split
strip

Read the words and look at the pictures. Circle the word that tells about each picture.

split
(string)
spring
strip

strange
sprang
splash
scratch

stream
spread
screw
street

split
splinter
strip
strike

street
scream
stream
spread

spray
scratch
strange
sprang

screech
spread
stream
street

splash
scratch
straight
sprang

spread
scream
stream
street

sprout
strong
scrap
stroke

spray
scrape
straw
splash

strange
scrape
splash
sprang

Symbol-sound association of words containing three-letter blends: spr, scr, spl, str

Three-Letter Blends

Name _____

Read each sentence and the words beside it. Write the word that makes sense in each sentence.

1. What a _____*strange*_____ day I've had today!

scratch
strange
sprang

2. I _____ a seam in my yellow shirt.

strike
split
strip

3. I _____ butter on my hand instead of on the toast.

stream
spread
scream

4. My best friend _____ his leg when we were playing.

stranger
sprained
screamed

5. I forgot to get a _____ for my milk when I went through the lunch line.

strange
straw
straight

6. The _____ on my only backpack broke.

splash
strap
scratch

7. I ran into the _____ door.

stream
screen
spread

8. I got a _____ in my right hand.

splinter
strip
strike

9. A car _____ water on me.

scraped
splashed
scratched

10. I think I'll go _____ to bed when I get home!

spray
scratch
straight

Words containing three-letter blends in context: spr, scr, spl, str

Three-Letter Blends

Name _____

Read the sentences. Complete the unfinished word in each sentence by writing the missing blend. Choose from the following blends: **spr, scr, spl, str.** You may use a blend more than once. The word you form must make sense in the sentence.

1. . Would you like to fix ___*scr*___ambled eggs for Grandmother?

2. Can Brenda swim _____aight across the deep end of the pool?

3. Try not to make a big _____ash when you dive.

4. I used the hose to _____ay water for the children.

5. Last spring I helped put a new _____een in my window.

6. How did Jan _____ain her arm?

7. We plan to plant some flowers next _____ing.

8. Before winter, we _____it wood to burn in our fireplace.

9. Before we begin painting the house, we must _____ape off the old paint.

10. Scott let out a loud _____eam when you frightened him.

11. Listen to that _____ange noise.

12. Is Allan _____ong enough to lift this box?

13. The first time Billy was up to bat, he got a _____ike.

14. How did you get that _____inter in your finger?

15. Are there any fish in that shallow _____eam?

Words containing three-letter blends in context: *spr, scr, spl, str*

Three-Letter Blends

Name _____

Read each clue. Complete the word beside it to form a word that matches the clue. Choose from the following blends: **spr, scr, spl, str.** You may use a blend more than once.

1. to hurt an arm or leg by twisting it — _spr_ain

2. not curved — _____aight

3. something cats do with their claws — _____atch

4. a wide brook — _____eam

5. to hurt the skin on a knee — _____ape

6. to wash with a brush — _____ub

7. what water does when you jump into a pool — _____ashes

8. something found in a barn — _____aw

9. a time of year when flowers bloom outdoors — _____ing

10. a tiny piece of wood — _____inter

11. another name for a road — _____eet

12. to yell in a high voice — _____eam

13. to put butter on bread — _____ead

14. to break something apart — _____it

15. to scatter tiny drops of water — _____ay

Review of words containing three-letter blends: *spr, scr, spl, str*

Ending Blends

Name _____

At the end of some words two consonants appear together. To say these words, blend the sounds of the two consonants together.

la**st**	sta**mp**
ha**nd**	g**ift**

Read the words and name the pictures. Circle the word that names each picture.

gasp (gift) golf gust		cast camp cent cost
mast mist mask milk		pink plant pump pant
rent raft ramp rest		bank bent bend band
stamp stand stump stunt		shelf shirt shift skunk

soft sand sink sent	
bump belt built best	
lamp left lump lift	
skunk skirt shift shirt	

40

Symbol-sound association of words containing final blends

Ending Blends

Name _____

Read each sentence and the words beside it. Write the word that makes sense in each sentence.

1. You need to put on old pants and a _____*shirt*_____.

shift
shirt
shelf

2. I want you to go with me to see what's _____ in the old barn.

lift
left
lamp

3. You can _____ me open the heavy sliding door.

honk
help
hand

4. I'll see if I can find a _____ to give us some light.

land
lamp
last

5. Look at the rusty tools on this _____.

short
shelf
shift

6. Do you think Grandfather used this tool to _____ seeds?

plant
part
paint

7. She wants to know what kind of bird _____ that nest.

belt
built
bold

8. We will have to _____ our teacher.

ask
ant
and

9. I can _____ him a letter tonight.

send
sent
self

10. Let's go to the old _____ on our next visit.

fast
fort
first

Ending Blends

Name _____

Complete the unfinished word in each sentence by writing the missing blends.
Choose from the following blends: **lf, lt, st, mp, nk, rt, ft, nd, nt, sk.** You may
use a blend more than once. The word you form must make sense in the sentence.

1. My friends met our family at the city airpo_*rt*___.

2. A strong wi_____ was blowing.

3. We ran to put the bags into the tru_____ of the car.

4. We stayed at my friend's home because we fe_____ it was too cold to camp.

5. First I put a funny ma_____ on my face.

6. Next I'll put on a wig made of so_____ yellow yarn.

7. I will wear a bright red shi_____ and baggy blue pants.

8. Then I'll be ready to go to work in the circus te_____.

9. Most of the books that tell how the old fo_____ was built have been sold.

10. There aren't many left on the she_____.

11. People must like the pictures drawn by the book's arti_____.

12. They sit at the de_____ in the bookstore and look at the books.

13. Please put a sta_____ on this letter.

14. I will se_____ it to Mom after we go swimming.

15. She will want to know about the ra_____ ride we took on the river.

Words containing final blends in context

Ending Blends

Name _____

Read each clue. Complete the word beside it to form a word that matches the clue. Choose from the following blends: **st, sk, nd, nk, nt, mp, lf, lt, rt, ft.** You may use a blend more than once.

1. a small lake — po*nd*

2. to spread color with a brush — pai_____

3. a tiny, make-believe person — e_____

4. what is left of a tree after it has been cut down — stu_____

5. a place to save money — ba_____

6. the part of the body that pumps blood — hea_____

7. the plaster covering on a broken arm or leg — ca_____

8. a present — gi_____

9. the opposite of right — le_____

10. something found at a beach — sa_____

11. a place for airplanes — airpo_____

12. a penny — ce_____

13. a group of people who play songs while marching — ba_____

14. a table used for writing or studying — de_____

15. a young male horse — co_____

Review of words containing final blends

Blends

Name _____

Read each set of sentences and its list of words. Write the word from the list that makes sense in each sentence.

1. Patty walks to the _____*pond*_____ in the park.

2. Her dog runs _____ her.

3. The dog likes to _____ water on itself.

4. Patty calls, and the dog runs _____ to her.

5. Patty _____ as her dog jumps up.

6. She throws a _____ into the air.

7. That dog likes to _____ "catch."

play
straight
squeals
stick
pond
splash
draw
past
plan

1. One day last week I was standing in _____ of the house.

2. I saw something _____ to move.

3. What was that _____ animal?

4. I moved slowly and tried to get _____ to it.

5. I was surprised to see a _____!

6. I've always been afraid of their _____.

7. "Oh, _____ don't let it spray me," I thought.

8. I was lucky that I didn't _____.

close
skunk
smell
free
front
scream
block
strange
start
please

Assessment of words containing initial and final blends in context

Name _____

In some words, two consonants together stand for one sound.
The letters **kn** usually stand for the sound of **n,** as in **knot.**
The letters **wr** usually stand for the sound of **r,** as in **write.**
The letters **sc** sometimes stand for the sound of **s,** as in **scissors.**

knot
write
scissors

Look at the pictures. Write the letters that stand for the beginning sound of each picture name.

_kn_ot

_____ientist

_____ee

_____ock

_____ap

_____it

_____ench

_____enery

_____inkle

_____ob

_____ite

_____issors

Sound-symbol association of words containing silent consonants: *kn, wr, sc*

Silent Consonants: *KN*, *WR*, and *SC*

Name _____

Read each sentence and the words beside it. Write the word that makes sense in each sentence.

1. I left my *science* book lying on the kitchen table.	science scene scent
2. What kind of _____ is good for cutting apples?	know knife knee
3. Who will be acting in the _____ that takes place in the garden?	scissors science scene
4. A _____ made of pine cones hangs on the front door.	wrote wren wreath
5. The bird in that tree is a _____.	write wren wreath
6. Please bring paper, pens, and _____ to art class.	scent scissors science
7. You will need to bring yellow yarn to the first _____ class.	kneeling knitting knocking
8. Can we _____ something as big as a bicycle?	wrap wrong wren
9. The people in the front row will _____ for the picture.	knew kneel know
10. Do you _____ how many people plan to come to the party?	know knit knock

Words containing silent consonants in context: *kn, wr, sc*

Silent Consonants: *KN, WR,* and *SC*

Name _____

Read each set of sentences and its list of words. Write the word from the list that makes sense in each sentence.

1. Arthur helped his brother get the _____*knot*_____ out of his shoelace.

2. When I finish _____ this box, we can go to the party.

3. My father _____ your mother when they were both children.

4. The _____ won a prize for her work.

5. I am afraid that I'll _____ my costume if I sit down.

6. Are those _____ sharp enough to cut this heavy paper?

knew

wrinkle

knot

scissors

wrong

wrapping

scientist

knowing

---

1. Was your mom able to put a new _____ on the door?

2. Is that a new watch I see on your _____?

3. Last week I bought a pair of _____ socks to go with my new skirt.

4. I have always liked smelling the _____ of roses.

5. Jennifer thought she heard a _____ at the door.

6. Did Cathy see the second _____ of the play?

scene

wrench

knob

knock

wrist

knee

wrong

scent

Silent Consonants: *CK, MB,* and *GH*

In some words, two consonants together stand for one sound. The letters **ck** usually stand for the sound of **k,** as in **duck.** The letters **mb** usually stand for the sound of **m,** as in **lamb.** The letters **gh** are usually silent, as in **night.**

du**ck**
la**mb**
ni**gh**t

Read the list of words below. Then look at the pictures. Write a word from the list that tells about each picture.

truck	eight	comb	climb	block
brick	light	clock	thumb	

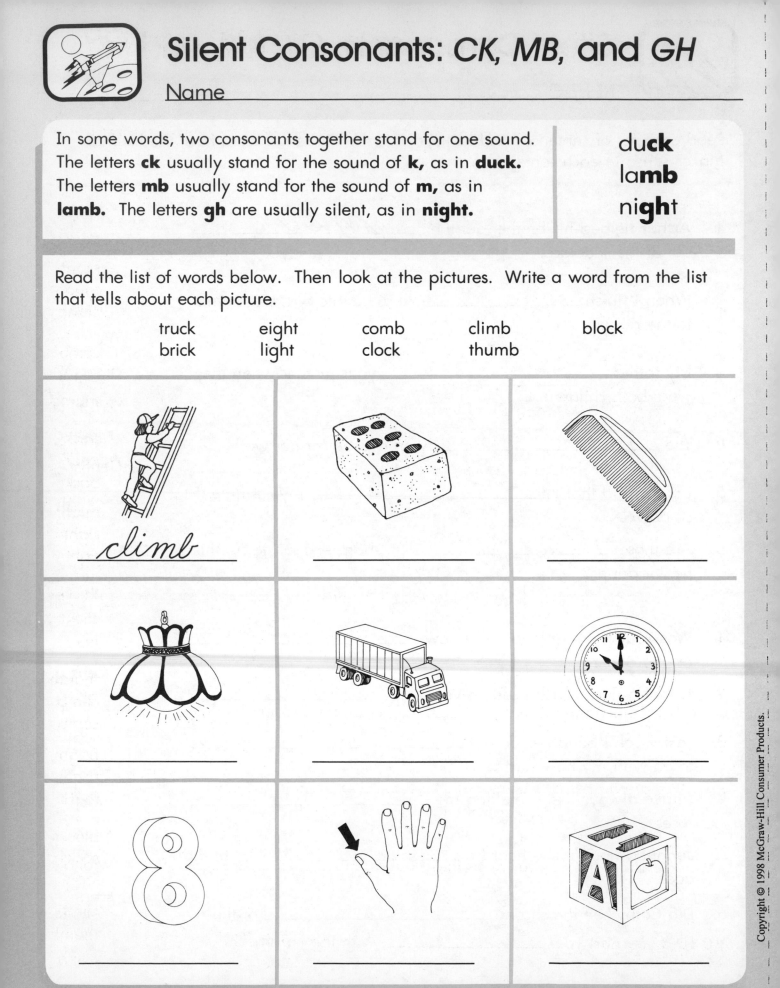

climb _____   _____   _____

_____   _____   _____

_____   _____   _____

Symbol-sound association of words containing silent consonants: *ck, mb, gh*

Silent Consonants: *CK, MB,* and *GH*

Name _____

Read each sentence and the words beside it. Write the word that makes sense in each sentence.

1. The little _*chicks*_ followed their mother.

sticks
chicks
thick

2. My teacher _____ Allen how to play the drums.

eight
taught
sight

3. Andrew will _____ his hair before his picture is taken.

comb
climb
thumb

4. How many times can you run around the _____?

pack
track
back

5. Our family _____ take a trip this summer.

might
sight
right

6. Before the grass is cut, we must walk around the yard and pick up each _____.

thick
stick
lick

7. Each fire fighter must _____ the ladder.

thumb
climb
comb

8. We ate dinner on our plane _____ to the city.

bright
fright
flight

9. The children have fun with these building _____.

blocks
socks
locks

10. Did you hurt your _____ with the hammer?

climb
thumb
comb

Silent Consonants: CK, MB, and GH

Read each set of sentences and its list of words. Write the word from the list that makes sense in each sentence.

1. I was able to hold a _____*lamb*_____ when I visited the zoo.

2. The new house is made of _____.

3. The little child covered with mud was quite a _____.

4. Do I have a hole in the toe of my _____?

5. Are you seven or _____ years old?

6. Jess plans on _____ that mountain.

7. Is the sun always so _____ in this window?

8. The dump _____ can carry a heavy load.

bright
sock
night
truck
lamb
thumb
eight
climbing
sight
bricks

---

1. In the winter, the birds eat the bread _____ we give them.

2. He was surprised when he _____ the ball.

3. We cannot ride our bicycles until it is _____ outside.

4. The gift was a brush and _____ set.

5. How _____ is the new downtown building?

6. Did you _____ to see that the lights are off?

7. We heard them _____ when the race was over.

comb
light
check
block
high
crumbs
sigh
climb
caught

Words containing silent consonants in context: ck, mb, gh

Silent Consonants

Name _____

Read each clue. Write **kn, wr, sc, ck, mb,** or **gh** to complete the word that matches the clue.

1. a time to sleep   ni_*gh*_t

2. painted scenes used in a play   _____enery

3. the flying of a plane or a jet   fli_____t

4. to make something with yarn   _____it

5. the part of the arm near the hand   _____ist

6. something used to make hair smooth   co_____

7. a baby sheep   la_____

8. the middle part of the leg   _____ee

9. a stone   ro_____

10. to put words down on paper   _____ite

11. not low   hi_____

12. something you do to get into a tree   cli_____

13. something a train moves on   tra_____

14. a tool used to tighten nuts and bolts   _____ench

15. the smell of something   _____ent

Review of words containing silent consonants: kn, wr, sc, ck, mb, gh

Silent Consonants

Name _____

Read the list of words below. Then read the sentences that follow. Write the word from the list that makes sense in each sentence.

crumbs	lock	knob	wrinkle	knock	science	wrap
quick	eight	scene	taught	thumb	straight	knew

1. If you ____*knock*____ three times, we'll let you into the clubhouse.

2. She twisted the _____ to turn on the television.

3. Danny painted a beautiful _____ of the mountains.

4. If we are _____, we can catch the morning train.

5. Aunt Joyce knew we had been eating because there were

   _____ on the table.

6. Be careful not to _____ your new shirt.

7. The children learned about plants in _____ class.

8. The holes in the scissors are for your finger and your _____.

9. Chee _____ his little sister how to tie her shoes.

10. What should Cindy use to _____ the food for our lunches?

11. This bicycle path goes _____ through the city.

12. So far, we have only _____ persons playing on our team.

13. Be sure to _____ the car door before you go shopping.

14. I _____ you would like reading that book.

Assessment of words containing silent consonants: *kn, wr, sc, ck, mb, gh*

Vowel Pairs: *AI, AY,* and *EI*

Name _____

In some words, two vowels together stand for one vowel sound. The letters **ai** and **ay** usually stand for the long-**a** sound, as in **train** and **hay**. The letters **ei** sometimes stand for the long-**a** sound, as in **eight**.

tr**ai**n
h**ay**
eight

Read the words and look at the pictures. Circle the word that tells about each picture.

sail **(train)** say tray	tray chain train chair	say sail stay sprain
braid trail brain tray	drain playground paint daisy	hay chain hair claim
wail stay weigh sail	sail say stay sleigh	fail vein faint veil
sprain stay spray stain	pay pail paint play	weight eight sleigh weigh

Symbol-sound association of words containing vowel digraphs: *ai, ay, ei*

Vowel Pairs: *AI, AY,* and *EI*

Name _____

Read each sentence and words beside it. Write the word that makes sense in each sentence.

1.	How long must we wait for the afternoon _____*train*_____?	tray tail train
2.	What kind of _____ do trains and planes carry?	reigns freight sleigh
3.	Can you teach me how to _____ my hair?	braid chain grain
4.	You can carry the dishes to the table on a _____.	train tray tail
5.	The nurse wrote my _____ on a chart.	freight weight sleigh
6.	Could you help me get the _____ out of the board?	nail sail tail
7.	The children liked the story about the well-known _____ that could fly.	reindeer freight weight
8.	Some people _____ water on their plants.	say straight spray
9.	Can you _____ at my house when your family goes away?	stain stay sleigh
10.	Do you know how to fix a bicycle _____?	braid chain train

Words containing vowel digraphs in context: *ai, ay, ei*

Vowel Pairs: *AI, AY,* and *EI*

Name _____

Read the list of words below. Then read the sentences that follow. Write the word from the list that makes sense in each sentence.

weight	crayons	daisy	playground	aim
stay	trail	sleigh	mail	highway
neighbor	eighteen	way		

1. We count cars when our family drives on the ___*highway*___.

2. Who will pick up your _____ at the post office when you are out of town?

3. You can score a point if you _____ the basketball at the rim.

4. Growing flowers is something my _____ does well.

5. If you walk on this dusty _____, you will come to Oak Lake.

6. Where will you _____ when you go on your trip to the city?

7. When it snows, Mrs. Bobbitt takes children on _____ rides through the woods.

8. You can find scissors, paper, and many _____ in my desk.

9. If you want to play kickball, meet on the school _____.

10. There are _____ boys and girls in that club.

11. Yoko put a _____ in her hair.

12. Which _____ should I turn when I get to the school?

13. As I grow taller, I will gain _____.

Vowel Pairs: *EE, EA, OA,* and *OW*

Name _____

In some words, two vowels together stand for one vowel sound. The letters **ee** usually stand for the long-**e** sound, as in **bee**. The letters **ea** can stand for the long-**e** sound, as in **bean** or the short-**e** sound, as in **bread**. The letters **oa** and **ow** often stand for the long-**o** sound, as in **coat** and **window**.

b**ee**
b**ea**n
br**ea**d
c**oa**t
wind**ow**

Read the words and name the pictures. Circle the word that names each picture.

beak (bee) bow boat	green goat grow groan	bowl bread boat beach
seek sneak snow seat	head heat heel heavy	loaf leaf lean low
sheep shadow show sheet	bee beak bread beach	boat beat bean bowl
three thread throat throw	row read roast road	tea teeth tree treat

Symbol-sound association of words containing vowel digraphs: *ee, ea, oa, ow*

Vowel Pairs: *EE, EA, OA,* and *OW*

Name _____

Read each sentence and the words beside it. Write the word that makes sense in each sentence.

1. Do you know how to tie a *bow* ?		bow beak bee
2. I fixed the _____ of my bicycle.		wheat wheel week
3. Would you like some butter or jelly on your _____?		toast team teeth
4. You may have some eggs for _____.		bread breakfast breath
5. Our basketball _____ works hard when it plays.		team tow teen
6. Today we'll have _____ and crackers for our snack.		cheek cheese cheap
7. The school nurse says I am very _____.		heats healthy heel
8. That dish can be cleaned with _____ and water.		soap seed seal
9. When my uncle sees me he always says, "My, how you've _____."		grown green greet
10. We will go swimming at the _____ behind our neighbor's house.		beak beach been

Words containing vowel digraphs in context: *ee, ea, oa, ow*

Vowel Pairs: *EE, EA, OA,* and *OW*

<u>Name</u>

Read the list of words below. Then read the sentences that follow. Write the word from the list that makes sense in each sentence.

need	teeth	heavy	show	bowl
reach	steep	float	goat	teacher
grow	meant	feather	roast	

1. Jane will be happy to ___*show*___ you her drawing.

2. We had fun feeding the playful _____ at the zoo.

3. The chart on the classroom wall was made by the _____.

4. We were careful when we climbed the _____ hill.

5. The basket of apples was too _____ for me to carry.

6. Justin _____ to call you this morning.

7. My little sister tried to _____ the books on the highest shelf.

8. When we were in the swimming pool, my dad showed me how to

_____.

9. The dentist checks my _____ twice a year.

10. Will I _____ eggs to make the muffins?

11. Let's put the popcorn in this yellow _____.

12. This daisy will _____ to be as tall as the fence.

13. I found a bird's _____ on the beach.

14. How long will it take to _____ the meat in this oven?

Words containing vowel digraphs in context: *ee, ea, oa, ow*

Vowel Pairs: *EE, EA, OA, and OW*

Name _____

Read each sentence and look at the vowel pairs beside it. Write one of the vowel pairs to complete the unfinished word in each sentence. The word you form must make sense in the sentence.

1. Put on your heavy c_*oa*_t before we go outside.   oa, ea

2. I can hear the wind bl_____ing.   ee, ow

3. Let's walk on this winding r_____d that leads to the barn.   oa, ee

4. We will give the horse a tr_____t.   ea, ow

5. The horse likes to eat _____ts from our hands.   ea, oa

6. Don't you think its fun to _____n a horse?   ow, ee

---

1. It's always pl_____sant to think about a summer trip.   oa, ea

2. I like to dr_____m about the many places I want to visit.   ea, ow

3. Sometime I'd like to take a long b_____t trip so I could see
   the sights.   ea, oa

4. I have always m_____nt to plan a train trip to the West.   ow, ea

5. The train I want to ride would have a place for me to sl_____p.   ee, ow

Vowel Pairs: *OO, AU, AW,* and *EW*

Name _____

In some words, two vowels together stand for one sound. The letters **oo** can stand for the sound you hear in the middle of **moon** or **book.** The letters **au** usually stand for the sound you hear at the beginning of **auto.** The letters **aw** usually stand for the sound you hear at the end of **saw.** The letters **ew** usually stand for the sound you hear in the middle of **news.**

m**oo**n
b**oo**k
auto
s**aw**
n**ew**s

Read the words and look at the pictures. Circle the word that tells about each picture.

(book) / boot / blew / broom	screw / school / straw / spoon	faucet / few / fault / flew
droop / draw / dew / dawn	claw / jaw / jewel / chew	hook / haul / hoop / hood
food / fool / flew / foot	lawn / look / launch / law	pool / straw / paw / spoon
saw / screw / soon / straw	blew / boot / book / brook	noon / blew / news / book

60

Vowel Pairs: OO, AU, AW, and EW

Name _____

Read each sentence and the words beside it. Write the word that makes sense in each sentence.

1. The light of the ___*moon*___ was bright last night.	mew moon moose
2. I believe there are a _____ tickets left for the show.	fawn few fault
3. Patrick _____ in the rain and waited for the bus.	spoon scoop stood
4. We will get up at _____ to catch the early morning train.	dawn dew draw
5. What kind of _____ should we make for the meat?	sauce screw straw
6. Colleen _____ a picture of the snowy mountains.	dew drew droop
7. Does that _____ crow every morning?	raccoon spoon rooster
8. The new speed _____ helps keep the highways safe.	look launch law
9. Marty hit a fly ball, and Benny _____ it.	caught claw cause
10. Richard _____ the coins out of his piggy bank.	shook straw sauce

Vowel Pairs: *OO, AU, AW,* and *EW*

Name _____

Read the list of words below. Then read the sentences that follow. Write the word from the list that makes sense in each sentence.

cause	look	yawn	flew	daughter
hawk	few	kangaroo	hook	taught
tooth	drawings	spoon	grew	

1. The baby needs a ___*spoon*___ for the food.

2. His little sister just lost a front _____.

3. I _____ when I get up too early in the morning.

4. Martin likes to make _____ of birds and flowers.

5. Please hang your coat on the _____ behind the door.

6. Can you tell me if that bird is a _____?

7. The princess is the _____ of the queen.

8. My aunt will _____ for a new car today.

9. My teacher _____ me how to add numbers.

10. Do you have a _____ minutes to listen to my tape?

11. When my family visited the zoo, my brother wanted to see a baby

    _____ in its mother's pouch.

12. Do the fire fighters know the _____ of the fire?

13. A hot-air balloon _____ over the fairgrounds this morning.

14. The farmers _____ more corn this year than last.

Words containing vowel digraphs in context: *oo, au, aw, ew*

Vowel Pairs: *OO, AU, AW,* and *EW*

Name _____

Read each sentence and look at the vowel pairs beside it. Write one of the vowel pairs to complete the unfinished word in each sentence. The word you form must make sense in the sentence.

1. There is much to do after sch__oo__l.   oo, au

2. You may plan to play baseball on the front l_____n.   aw, ew

3. The swimming p_____l is open.   oo, au

4. You can check out a b_____k from the library.   oo, aw

5. You'll need to p_____se and think about what you'd like to do.   au, oo

---

1. One day we got up at d_____n.   aw, oo

2. A f_____ of us quickly got dressed.   aw, ew

3. We had planned a walk in the w_____ds.   oo, au

4. Our leader had t_____ght us about animal tracks.   oo, au

5. Before long, Danny s_____ some small tracks.   oo, aw

6. We were following a family of racc_____ns.   au, oo

Words containing vowel digraphs in context: *oo, au, aw, ew*

Vowel Pairs

Name _____

Read the list of words below. Then read the sentences that follow. Write the word from the list that makes sense in each sentence.

bread	train	stay	speak	steep	soon	keep
book	draw	few	jewel	own	road	drew

1. I would like to make some _____*bread*_____ for my neighbor.

2. Can you _____ here awhile and help me bake a loaf?

3. I need a map that shows the _____ where the shops are.

4. Please _____ the map with a marker on this sheet of paper.

5. Will you _____ these tickets for me until I'm ready to go?

6. I will be taking a _____ ride into the city to see your daughter.

7. Nancy got a _____ from the library today.

8. Someday she would like to have her _____ set of books.

9. My aunt and uncle have a _____ horses and cows.

10. They will also have sheep at their ranch _____.

11. Andrew _____ a picture of a fancy crown.

12. A beautiful _____ was in the center of the crown.

13. Are you able to _____ to the group at this week's meeting?

14. We would like to hear about the _____ mountain you climbed.

Review of words containing vowel digraphs in context: *ai, ay, ee, ea, oa, ow, oo, aw, ew*

Tie has the long-**i** sound spelled by the letters **ie**. Shield has the long-**e** sound spelled by the letters **ie**.

tie   **shield**

Read the words and look at the pictures. Circle the word that tells about each picture.

(tie)
lie

die
pie

lie
necktie

field
lie

niece
movie

chief
thief

field
movie

die
chief

piece
die

cookie
tie

piece
pie

field
shield

Symbol-sound association of words containing *ie*

Vowel Pairs: *IE*

Name _____

Read the list of words. Notice the sound that **ie** stands for in each word. Then write each word under the correct heading.

tie **shield**

field	lie	niece	thief
necktie	pie	die	movie

Long i as in tie

necktie

_____

_____

_____

Long e as in shield

_____

_____

_____

_____

Read the sentences. Complete each sentence by writing a word from the exercise above. The word you write must make sense in the sentence.

1. His *necktie* matched the color of his jacket.

2. We like to pick wild flowers from the _____ near our home.

3. Would you like to _____ down and rest?

4. Her family watched an exciting _____ about runners.

5. What made that plant _____?

6. My _____ has a beautiful smile.

7. The _____ had taken the important papers.

Symbol-sound association of words containing *ie*; Words containing *ie* in context

Vowel Pairs: *IE*

Name _____

Read the sentences and the list of words. Write the word
from the list that makes sense in each sentence.

tie   **shield**

1. Mindy will _____*tie*_____ string around the box.

2. I would like to be the _____ of the fire fighters.

3. I _____ you can run the race faster than you
   ever have before.

4. Should my dad wear a _____ tonight?

5. The grass will _____ if it doesn't get enough
   water.

6. Have you ever told a _____?

7. May I have another _____ of paper?

8. The teacher showed a _____ after we talked
   about the city.

9. The police are looking for the _____ who ran
   out of the bank with the money.

10. I have been an aunt since my _____ Kris
    was born.

11. The team can play softball in that _____.

12. Each knight in the painting is holding a heavy

    _____.

chief

shield

die

piece

niece

necktie

thief

lie

field

believe

movie

tie

Words containing *ie* in context

Vowel Pairs: OU

Name _____

In some words, two vowels together stand for one vowel sound. The letters **ou** can stand for the vowel sounds you hear in **soup** and **should.**

sou**p**
shou**ld**

Read the list of words. Notice the sound that **ou** stands for in each word. Write each word under the correct heading.

| group | wouldn't | could | through | coupon |
| would | shouldn't | youth | couldn't | you |

ou as in **soup**   **ou** as in **should**

group _____   _____

_____   _____

_____   _____

_____   _____

Read the sentences and the word choices. Circle the word that makes sense in each sentence.

1. Grandmother told me I (through, (should)) remember to wear my coat.

2. (Wouldn't, Youth) it be nice to have a picture of that sunset?

3. We save money by using (should, coupons) when we shop.

4. A (group, couldn't) of six children will play on each team.

5. Our teacher told us we (coupon, could) write a story.

6. What kind of (should, soup) do I smell cooking?

7. We will hike over the hill and (would, through) the woods.

Vowel Pairs: *OU*

Name _____

In some words, two vowels together stand for one vowel sound. The letters **ou** can stand for the vowel sounds you hear in **touch** and **doughnut**.

touch
doughnut

Read the list of words. Notice the sound that **ou** stands for in each word. Write each word under the correct heading.

| double | couple | dough | southern | shoulder |
| enough | although | young | though | |

ou as in **touch**

double

_____

_____

_____

ou as in **doughnut**

_____

_____

_____

Read the sentences and the word choices. Circle the word that makes sense in each sentence.

1. Have you ever tasted bread ((dough), double) like this?

2. Debbie knows how to make whole wheat (double, doughnuts).

3. Would you like to visit my uncle in the (country, couple)?

4. Jennie's (cousin, though) can make flutes out of wood.

5. The player who made a (touchdown, through) jumped up and down.

6. I put the backpack over my (southern, shoulder).

7. Do you have (enough, although) wood to build a fire?

Symbol-sound association of words containing *ou*; Words containing *ou* in context

Read the story. Circle each word that contains **ou.** Then answer the questions that follow. There are twenty-three words that contain **ou.**

(Though) we had never done it before, our youth group planned to make bread. We should have started with something easy, but we like bread! We went through the food store with many coupons, buying enough for an army.

Jan wanted us to get double of everything on our list. Doug had to carry a large bag of flour over his shoulder. The shopkeeper said it looked as if we were going to open a shop with all of the bread we planned to make.

The next day we all met at the home of Jan's cousin. Our plan was to first mix a little bit of the dough. We didn't have any trouble. Before long, we had baked a beautiful loaf of bread. We spent the rest of the day baking bread. By the time we were through, we had enough for each of us to take a loaf home.

I shared my bread with my family. My dad said, "The group you belong to is young, but they surely know how to bake." He should know. He ate five pieces!

Use the story to answer the questions.

1. What word from the first paragraph rhymes with **dough?** ___*though*___

2. What kind of group baked the bread? _____

3. What did the group take to the store in order to save money? _____

4. What word from the second paragraph means "twice as much"? _____

5. How did Doug carry the flour? _____

6. What word from the third paragraph means "finished"? _____

Identifying words containing *ou;* Words containing *ou* in context

Vowel Pairs

Name _____

Read the list of words below. Then read the sentences that follow. Write the word from the list that makes sense in each sentence.

necktie	field	dough	would	should
chief	enough	tie	believe	
route	touch	movie	through	

1. I have never worn a _____necktie_____ before.

2. Will you show me how to _____ it?

3. What _____ I do without your help?

4. We can make this _____ into bread or rolls.

5. There may be _____ of the mix to make both.

6. Let's taste the bread as soon as we're _____.

7. This is the _____ shown on the map that we should follow.

8. It will take us past a _____ of corn.

9. Can you _____ that covered wagons once used this road?

10. Would you and your brother like to see a good _____?

11. The show is about a well-known Indian _____.

12. The zoo worker said that some snakes _____ be fed every day.

13. She asked us if we'd like to _____ the skin of a snake.

Two Sounds of Y

When **y** comes at the end of a word that has no other vowel, the **y** usually stands for the long-**i** sound as in **fly**. When **y** comes at the end of a word that has another vowel, the **y** usually stands for the long-**e** sound as in **pony**.

fl**y**   pon**y**

Read the words and look at the pictures. Circle the word that tells about each picture.

fly
(jelly)

spy
puppy

carry
cry

dry
daisy

fly
funny

fry
forty

sky
snowy

try
rainy

funny
fry

daisy
dry

silly
sky

rocky
cry

Symbol-sound association of words containing *y* as a vowel

Two Sounds of Y

Name _____

Read the words below. Write **long e** or **long i** next to each word to show the sound that **y** stands for.

fl**y** pon**y**

1. fly   *long i*
2. angry   _____
3. sixty   _____
4. why   _____
5. dry   _____
6. thirsty _____

7. stormy _____
8. shy   _____
9. lucky   _____
10. fry   _____
11. empty _____
12. cry   _____

Read the sentences and the word choices. Circle the word that makes sense in each sentence.

1. Tommy will (try, fry) to answer each of your questions.

2. Can you get me a (carry, copy) of the story you read to us today?

3. We can go sled riding on the first (sixty, snowy) day.

4. When I learned that my best friend was moving, I began to (dry, cry).

5. Should we buy a pack of twenty or (rainy, forty) paper plates for the party?

6. On the day we began our trip there wasn't a cloud in the (shy, sky).

7. Are those math books too (heavy, healthy) for you to carry?

8. I'd like to know (shy, why) the date of the football game was changed.

Two Sounds of Y

Name _____

fl**y**   pon**y**

Read the list of words. Notice the sound that **y** stands for in each word. Write each word under the correct heading.

| try | sky | sixty | stormy | fry |
| cry | penny | rocky | shiny | shy |

Long i as in fly

try

_____

_____

_____

_____

Long e as in pony

_____

_____

_____

_____

Read the sentences. Complete each sentence by writing a word from the exercise above. The word you write must make sense in the sentence.

1. Would you like to _____*try*_____ to fly my new kite?

2. We climbed up the steep, _____ hillside.

3. Will that school bus hold more than _____ children?

4. Have you ever tried to count each star in the _____?

5. Uncle Richard can bake or _____ the fish in a pan for you.

6. Aunt Janie's new _____ bicycle is silver.

Vowel Pairs and Sounds of Y

Name _____

Read the list of words below. Then read the sentences that follow. Write the word from the list that makes sense in each sentence.

try	taught	weight	raccoon	healthy
field	trail	cousin	cheese	straw
toast	chew	window	through	

1. We should ___*try*___ to get together to play basketball.

2. I would like two eggs and some _____ with jam this morning.

3. The farmer carried a bale of _____ into the barn.

4. The nurse always checks the baby's _____ on the scales.

5. Dennis _____ us how to use a rowboat.

6. What kind of _____ should I put on this sandwich?

7. Mandy's puppy likes to _____ toy bones.

8. We can fly kites from the grassy _____.

9. Eating good food helps you stay _____.

10. I wish my _____ could go shopping with us.

11. Every year the hiking _____ is used by many people.

12. I never rode _____ a tunnel.

13. If you look out this _____, you can see the lights of the city.

14. Did you see that _____ walking on our picnic table?

Assessment of words containing vowel digraphs and of words containing *y* as a vowel in context

Name _____

City Workers

Many people in the city work to help us. They do things for us that we cannot do for ourselves.

Police

Police officers help us in many ways. They help people cross the street safely. They help little children find their way if they are lost. They find people who break the law. They make our cities safe to live in.

Mail Carriers

Mail carriers bring letters and newspapers to people's homes. They also bring books, toys, and clothes that we have sent away for. They do their work in sun, snow, rain, or wind.

Fire Fighters

Fire fighters are ready at all times to fight fires. They put out fires in homes and other buildings. They save people's lives. They go to schools to teach children about fire safety.

1. Check the answer that tells the main idea.

    _____ people who help us

    _____ what people can do to help the police

    _____ how to fight fires

2. Write two things that fire fighters do.

    _____

    _____

Name _____

3. Write the name of the worker under each picture.

_____   _____   _____

4. In what way are a police officer and a fire fighter the same?

_____

5. Tell how your life might be different without one of these city workers.

        police   mail carriers   fire fighters

_____

_____

_____

6. Choose one of these city workers. Tell how this person helps people in the city.

      bus driver   mayor   lifeguard   street cleaner

_____

_____

_____

_____

Application of thinking and writing skills in a social studies context

Consonant Pairs

Name _____

Two consonants together can stand for one sound. Some consonants that stand for one sound are **sh, ch, th,** and **wh.** At the beginning of some words, three consonants together stand for a special sound as in **three.**

shoe	**wh**eel
chair	**thr**ee
thin	

Name the pictures. Write the letters that stand for the beginning sound in each picture name.

_thr_ead	_____ovel	_____irteen
_____ain	_____eel	_____imney

Read the sentences. Complete the unfinished word in each sentence by writing the missing letters. Choose from the following consonant pairs. **sh, ch, th, wh, thr.** You may use a consonant pair more than once.

1. My dog looks like a puppy, but he is _____*thr*____ee years old.

2. When he was a puppy, he would drag my old _____ite shirt around.

3. Sometimes he would hide it under a _____air.

4. Do you know that he is still afraid of his own _____adow?

5. I like to _____ow a ball for him to catch.

6. I _____ink my dog is great fun to watch!

Sound-symbol association of words containing initial consonant digraphs; Words containing initial consonant digraphs in context: *sh, ch, th, wh, thr*

Consonant Pairs

Name _____

Read each sentence and the words beside it. Write the word that makes sense in each sentence.

1. If you get some ___*thread*___, I will fix your coat.

   cheese
   thread
   shed

2. I always lay my glasses on this _____.

   three
   shelf
   check

3. In art class, we form clay into many different _____.

   shapes
   change
   thanks

4. The police believe that a _____ tried to break into the bank.

   thief
   whip
   chin

5. I will read my book _____ you talk to the man who works in the children's library.

   child
   while
   shield

6. Are there any sea animals bigger than a _____?

   chain
   shake
   whale

7. Is there a _____ that you'll be able to go swimming with me?

   shark
   than
   chance

8. The queen sat on a _____ to receive her crown.

   shook
   throne
   choke

9. Our group would like to _____ you for your help with the play.

   thank
   chain
   shadow

10. Before we build a fire, let's have the _____ cleaned.

    thirteen
    chimney
    whistle

Words containing initial consonant digraphs in context: *sh, ch, th, wh, thr*

79

Ending Consonant Pairs

Name _____

At the end of a word, two or three consonants together can stand for one sound. Some consonants that stand for one sound are **sh, ch, tch, th,** and **ng.**

wi**sh**　　wi**th**
ea**ch**　　ri**ng**
ca**tch**

Name the pictures. Write the letters that stand for the ending sound in each picture name.

pea**ch**　　　wa_____　　　bru_____

tee_____　　　ben_____　　　stri_____

Read the sentences. Complete the unfinished word in each sentence by writing the letters that stand for the ending sound. Choose from the following consonant pairs: **sh, ch, tch, th, ng.** You may use a consonant pair more than once. The word you form must make sense in the sentence.

1. Please come alo___*ng*___ with Callie and me.

2. Bo_____ of us would like you to join the baseball team.

3. Today the coach will tea_____ us how to pitch.

4. Next week we will learn more about how to ca_____ the ball.

5. We'll have to ru_____ if we want to be at the field on time.

Sound-symbol association of words containing final consonant digraphs; Words containing final consonant digraphs in context: *sh, ch, tch, th, ng*

Ending Consonant Pairs

Name _____

Read each sentence and the words beside it. Write the word that makes sense in each sentence.

1. The band will ___*march*___ onto the field and play the school song.

match
math
march

2. This morning we bought enough _____ for two kites.

scratch
splash
string

3. A large _____ was broken off our elm tree during the storm.

both
brush
branch

4. The picture will turn out better if you use a _____ on your camera.

flash
splash
crash

5. How many _____ does the baby have now?

teach
teeth
leash

6. When the bell _____, the children hurried from the playground to the classroom.

ranch
rash
rang

7. Our sleds made a _____ through the snowy woods.

path
patch
peach

8. The _____ on this lamp is broken.

switch
such
swing

9. The kitten didn't mean to _____ you.

spring
scratch
sang

10. When I visit my cousins' farm, I like to _____ the horses.

branch
booth
brush

Words containing final consonant digraphs in context: sh, ch, tch, th, ng

81

Consonant Pairs

Name _____

The letters **gh** sometimes stand for the sound of **f,** as in lau**gh.** The letters **ph** usually stand for the sound of **f,** as in ele**ph**ant.

lau**gh**   ele**ph**ant

Read the words and look at the pictures. Circle the word that tells about each picture.

(photo)   alphabet   phone

tough   laughing   cough

tough   laugh   enough

telephone   photo   elephant

Read the sentences and the word choices. Circle the word that makes sense in each sentence.

1. Will you answer the (telephone, rough) while I am reading?

2. When we drive our car over the (phone, rough) road, we bounce on the seats.

3. Sammy likes to take (laugh, photos) when he's on a trip.

4. When you visited the zoo, did you see the baby (elephant, rough)?

5. The meat is too (phone, tough) to cut with this knife.

6. Does Sandy have (enough, telephone) paper for art class?

7. Rosa makes faces to make the baby (laugh, photo).

Symbol-sound association of words containing consonant digraphs;
Words containing consonant digraphs in context: *gh, ph*

Consonant Pairs

Name _____

Read the list of words below. Then read the sentences that follow. Write the word from the list that makes sense in each sentence.

tough	elephant	telephone	alphabet
laugh	enough	rough	nephew
microphone	rougher	photograph	laughing

1. You may want to use a _microphone_ when you speak to large groups.

2. Will Brad have _____ time to visit us this week?

3. Dad is teaching Sue the letters of the _____.

4. I know you'll _____ when you read this funny story.

5. Because the wood of the chair is _____, we'll use sandpaper to make it smooth.

6. My sister is my aunt's niece, and my brother is her

   _____.

7. The children were _____ at the circus clown.

8. I am sorry that the meat I cooked is so _____.

9. This road is _____ than it was last winter.

10. I can't hear the _____ ringing when I'm working outside.

11. Ann wants to give me a _____ of her cats.

12. Val has always wanted to feed peanuts to an _____.

Consonant Pairs

Name _____

Read the list of words below. Then read the clues that follow. Write the word from the list that matches each clue.

rough	tough	laugh	telephone	photo
nephew	enough	alphabet	elephant	

1. not smooth _____ *rough*

2. what you do when you think something is funny _____

3. a boy who has an aunt or uncle _____

4. starts with **a, b, c** _____

5. as much as is needed _____

6. something you can use to talk with another person _____

7. hard to chew or cut _____

8. a picture that is taken with a camera _____

9. a large circus animal _____

Read the sentences and the word choices. Circle the word that makes sense in each sentence.

1. Her little sister knows the letters of the (alphabet, elephant).

2. Please answer the (tough, telephone) for me.

3. The bark of that tree feels very (rough, laugh).

4. I would like to see the (enough, photos) you took with your camera.

5. The jokes in your book made me (nephew, laugh).

84

Consonant Pairs

Name _____

Read each clue. Write **sh, ch, wh, ng,** or **gh** to complete the word that matches the clue.

1. a food made from milk   ___*ch*___eese

2. something you blow into that makes a high noise   _____istle

3. a tool used for digging   _____ovel

4. two pieces of bread with meat between them   sandwi_____

5. a playground toy you can sit on   swi_____

6. hard to cut   tou_____

7. something you make when you jump into water   spla_____

Read each clue. Write **th, ph, thr,** or **tch** to complete the word that matches the clue.

1. something that can feel sore when you have a cold   ___*thr*___oat

2. a number greater than two   _____ee

3. a picture taken with a camera   _____oto

4. a part of your hand   _____umb

5. a piece of cloth that covers a hole in a piece of clothing   pa_____

6. something that is used to make clothes   clo_____

7. something used to light a candle   ma_____

Consonant Pairs

Name _____

Read each set of sentences and its list of words. Write the word from the list that makes sense in each sentence.

1. My family likes to ___*watch*___ parades.

2. We always go early so that we can sit on a _____.

3. The last parade we saw had _____ marching bands.

4. I clapped as I saw each one _____ by.

5. When I knew the tunes, I would _____ along.

6. I was surprised to see a float being pulled by an

    _____.

7. If I were in a parade, the children would

    _____ at my funny clown costume.

march
laugh
thumb
watch
elephant
bench
sing
thirty
catch

---

1. I _____ this room looked nicer.

2. I wonder if I should paint the walls _____.

3. Should I keep _____ the lamp and the basket on that table?

4. Shall I put two or _____ pictures on this wall?

5. Where should I hang this _____ for my books?

6. Please tell me what you _____ about this chair.

7. Did I hear you say, "Don't _____ a thing"?

shelf
both
wish
whisper
three
white
shake
change
think

Assessment of words containing initial and final consonant digraphs in context

Vowels With *R*

Name _____

When a vowel is followed by the letter **r,** the vowel stands for a special sound that is neither long nor short. For example, **ar** stands for the sound you hear in **jar; er, ir,** and **ur** stand for the sounds you hear in **fern, bird,** and **burn; or** stands for the sound you hear in **horn.**

j**ar**	h**or**n
f**er**n	b**ur**n
b**ir**d	

Name the pictures and read the sentences. Circle the word in each sentence that has the same vowel sound as the picture name.

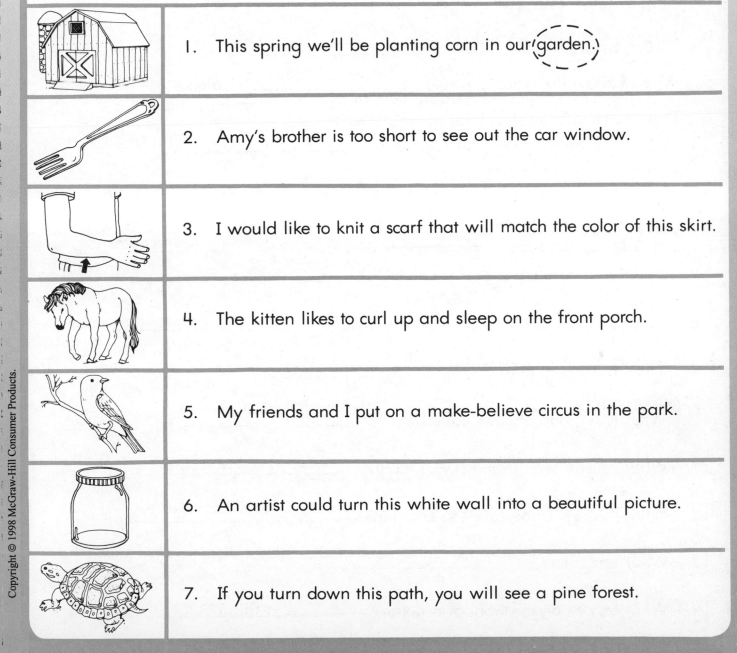

1. This spring we'll be planting corn in our garden.

2. Amy's brother is too short to see out the car window.

3. I would like to knit a scarf that will match the color of this skirt.

4. The kitten likes to curl up and sleep on the front porch.

5. My friends and I put on a make-believe circus in the park.

6. An artist could turn this white wall into a beautiful picture.

7. If you turn down this path, you will see a pine forest.

Sound-symbol association of words containing *r*-controlled vowels

Vowels With *R*

Name _____

Read the list of words below. Then read the questions that follow. Write the word from the list that answers each question.

turkey	porch	nurse	storm	stars
scarf	dirt	forest	slippers	herd
purple	thirty	card	ladder	

1. What is a large bird?   *turkey*

2. In what is a seed planted? _____

3. What brings snow or rain? _____

4. What can you sign and send in the mail? _____

5. What can be worn on your feet? _____

6. What can you wear to keep your head or neck

   warm? _____

7. Who helps care for people who are ill? _____

8. What can you use to climb to high places? _____

9. What has many trees? _____

10. What is a group of cows called? _____

11. What can be seen in the sky at night? _____

12. What number comes after twenty-nine? _____

13. What is a color? _____

14. What can be on the front of a house? _____

Words containing *r*-controlled vowels in context

Vowels With *R*

Name _____

Read the sentences and the word choices. Circle the word that makes sense in each sentence.

1. I go to the craft center with my friends each Saturday (morning, market).

2. The (teachers, torch) show us a different craft every week.

3. One time, we made little (lanterns, large) out of tin.

4. Another time, I used a new kind of paint to color a white (shirt, sharp).

5. I have made a scarf out of yarn and a belt out of (ladder, leather).

6. Sometimes I make mistakes, but most of my things (torn, turn) out all right.

7. My work at the center makes me want to become an (artist, other).

---

1. Last night's storm made a mess of our (yard, yarn).

2. Now we must try to save the plants in our (germ, garden).

3. Our tall green corn plants are now lying in the (dirt, dart).

4. I'll use a broom to sweep the front (perch, porch).

5. My older brother and my (sister, squirrel) will get the tree branches off the roof.

6. We are lucky that the storm did not (her, hurt) the apple tree we just planted.

7. I hope the wind doesn't blow so (hard, horn) in the next storm.

Words containing *r*-controlled vowels in context

Vowels With *R*

<u>Name</u>_____

Read each sentence and look at the letter pairs beside it. Write one of the letter pairs to complete the unfinished word in each sentence. The word you form must make sense in the sentence.

1. We planted rows of seeds in the g_*ar*_den.   ar, er

2. I like to watch the dancer t_____n when he dances on the stage.   or, ur

3. The tail of the squ_____rel is bushy.   ar, ir

4. Before it snows, we will cov_____ the plants in our garden.   or, er

5. A sales cl_____k will be able to help you find a shirt in your size.   er, or

6. We put our bikes in the shed when it began to st_____m.   ur, or

7. I feed my t_____tle once a day in the morning.   or, ur

8. There are seats for f_____ty children in the classroom.   ir, or

9. We buy our eggs and milk at a f_____m.   or, ar

10. You'll find the answ_____ to your question in this book.   or, er

11. Shane would like to try out for a p_____t in the play.   ir, ar

12. The hamm_____ hit my thumb instead of the nail.   er, ar

13. This ch_____t shows how far I have run this spring.   ar, or

14. Carla has my comb in her p_____se.   ar, ur

15. The group must form a c_____cle before the game begins.   ar, ir

90

Vowels With *R*

Name _____

Read the sentences and the list of words. Write the word from the list that makes sense in each sentence.

1. A ___*turtle*___ is a good pet to keep in a small home.

2. There are twelve fresh eggs in the _____.

3. The balloon made a loud noise when it _____.

4. That pile of _____ must be moved before the building begins.

5. The artist uses gold and _____ to make bracelets.

6. My baby brother is too _____ to reach the doorknob.

7. Which runner do you think will be the _____ to cross the finish line?

8. Please pass the salt and _____ shakers to me.

9. What kind of wood will _____ best in a fireplace?

10. Sometimes my dog _____ when I won't let her come outside with me.

11. Our class will hear a _____ talk about her trip to Spain.

12. My older sister lives in an _____ near our house.

13. I know spring is near when I hear the birds _____.

14. The puppy was _____ three weeks ago.

burn

first

chirp

pepper

silver

apartment

dirt

burst

speaker

born

turtle

barks

short

carton

Review of words containing *r*-controlled vowels in context

Vowels With R

Name _____

Read the list of words below. Then read the sentences that follow. Write the word from the list that makes sense in each sentence.

porch	better	squirrels	thirty
hurry	alarm	slippers	birthday
parking	forget	horse	hurt

1. After school I come home and sit on the front _____*porch*_____ .

2. I like to watch the _____ run through the trees.

3. They make me _____ the cares of my day.

4. Don takes lessons to learn how to ride a _____ .

5. His teacher says that Don's riding is getting _____ every week.

6. I'll be going to Kate's surprise _____ party next week.

7. The party will be held at the park behind the school _____ lot.

8. I must _____ to get to the post office.

9. The mail will be picked up there in _____ minutes.

10. I jumped out of bed when the _____ rang this morning.

11. One of my _____ fell off as I ran down the hallway.

12. I'm surprised I didn't _____ myself as I hurried through the house.

Assessment of words containing *r*-controlled vowels in context

OI, OY, OU, and OW

Name _____

The letters **oi** and **oy** stand for the vowel sounds in **coin** and **toys**. The letters **ou** and **ow** often stand for the vowel sounds you hear in **cloud** and **cow**.

coin   **clou**d
toys   **cow**

Read the list of words below. Then look at the pictures. Write a word from the list that tells about each picture.

cloud   point   frown   boy   boil   bounce

cloud _____ _____

_____ _____ _____

Read the sentences and the word choices. Circle the word that makes sense in each sentence.

1. Last weekend my cousin and I were looking (around, allow) his basement.

2. We (foil, found) a trunk that was full of old picture books.

3. One book had a picture of a different circus (cloud, clown) on each page.

4. Another book had drawings of beautiful (flowers, found).

5. My cousin's mother told me I could have my (crowd, choice) of the old books.

6. I (join, enjoy) looking at the book about animals that I took home.

OI, OY, OU, and OW

Name _____

Read each sentence and the words beside it. Write the word that makes sense in each sentence.

1. My neighbor's little _____*boy*_____ likes to ride his bicycle on the bike path.

   boil
   boy

2. My sister can name the different kinds of _____ in the sky.

   clouds
   coins

3. Every child in that family has a beautiful singing

   _____.

   voice
   vow

4. The _____ princess told the children a story.

   royal
   round

5. We learned that some plants can have _____ in them.

   pound
   poison

6. Rose tries to see how high the basketball will _____.

   boiling
   bounce

7. I would like to take a picture of the sand castle before the

   waves _____ it.

   down
   destroy

8. Is this dark _____ good for growing corn?

   scout
   soil

9. When we walked through the barn, I saw a _____ run across the floor.

   mouse
   mouth

10. The young girl _____ when she lost her balloon.

   frowned
   found

94

Words containing diphthongs in context: oi, oy, ou, ow

OI, OY, OU, and OW

Name _____

Read the clues and the list of words. Write the word from the list that matches each clue.

1. something that helps to keep machines running   _____*oil*_____

2. sounds   _____

3. to yell   _____

4. a large bird   _____

5. a farm tool that loosens dirt   _____

6. things that children play with   _____

7. a group of many people   _____

8. to hit with a hammer   _____

9. something that water does when it is very hot   _____

10. dirt   _____

11. the sharp end of something   _____

12. the part of the face used to smile   _____

13. a very tall building   _____

14. a young man   _____

15. a sea animal that lives in a shell   _____

pound

oil

shout

tower

plow

soil

noises

point

boy

toys

boils

crowd

mouth

owl

oyster

OI, OY, OU, and OW

Name _____

Read each sentence and look at the letter pairs beside it. Write one of the letter pairs to complete the unfinished word in each sentence. The word you form must make sense in the sentence.

1. I will see if Dad will all_**ow**_ me to take the bus.   ow, oi

2. I would like to ride to t_____n with my friend Beth.   oy, ow

3. If we go right after school, there will be no cr_____ds in the stores.   ow, oy

4. Beth knows how to get ar_____nd from one place to another.   ou, oi

5. She will help me find a t_____ for Timmy's birthday.   oy, ou

6. We will go to a shop that sells stamps and c_____ns.   ow, oi

7. Beth thinks I will enj_____ looking in the other store windows, too.   ou, oy

8. We are planning to return to Beth's h_____se before it gets dark.   oi, ou

1. Last spring I wanted to j_____n an outdoors club.   oi, ow

2. My friend Joy told me about being a sc_____t.   oi, ou

3. I would enj_____ being a member of the group.   oy, ou

4. Our hike up Snowball M_____ntain was one I'll never forget.   ou, oi

5. The hike back d_____n to our campsite was not easy because the mountain paths are steep.   oi, ow

6. I am pr_____d to be a part of the group.   ou, oi

Words containing diphthongs in context: *oi, oy, ou, ow*

OI, OY, OU, and OW

Name _____

Read the sentences and the word choices. Circle the word that makes sense in each sentence.

1. Flowers will grow well in this rich (sound, (soil))

2. The singer works hard to make his (voice, choice) sound better.

3. When I went shopping, I bought eggs, milk, and a bag of (frown, flour).

4. Martha and Sandra are building a tall (tower, powder) of blocks.

5. The princess doll wears a golden (count, crown) on her head.

6. I like to (bounce, bow) the ball when I am on the school playground.

7. I have learned how to check the (out, oil) in our family car.

8. What kind of bath (toys, town) do babies like best?

9. When you are so far away, I can hear you only if you (shower, shout).

10. My dog will (ground, growl) if he hears a strange noise.

11. The scientist can check for (poisons, pound) in a plant.

12. I saw an (oil, oyster) shell when I visited the beach.

13. An older friend taught me how to (pound, powder) a nail into a board.

14. The beautiful horses belong to the queen and her (royal, voice) family.

15. The white, fluffy (clown, clouds) look pretty in the blue sky.

16. She has lived in this (town, toy) since she was a young girl.

17. A little gray (mouth, mouse) ran across the barn.

18. Put the corn into the pan after the water begins to (boil, bow).

Review of words containing diphthongs in context: oi, oy, ou, ow

OI, OY, OU, and OW

Name _____

Read the list of words below. Then read the sentences that follow. Write the word from the list that makes sense in each sentence.

ouch	clown	point	pound
frowning	boil	out	towel
boys	enjoy	join	choice

1. Let me know when the water in the pan starts to ___*boil*___.

2. I have more than one _____ of green beans to cook.

3. My family will _____ eating something from our garden.

4. Do you know why I am _____?

5. I just fell _____ of that small oak tree.

6. I am not hurt, but I did yell "_____" when I landed.

7. My sister has fun when she dresses up as a _____.

8. She says it's fun to make girls and _____ smile.

9. Please _____ to the row you would like to sit in.

10. Today you can have your _____ of seats.

11. Will you _____ me when I go to the beach to swim?

12. Don't forget your sunglasses and a _____.

Assessment of words containing diphthongs in context: *oi, oy, ou, ow*

Endings: -ED and -ING

Name _____

walk	walk**ing**
snap	snapp**ed**

Many new words can be formed by adding **-ed** or **-ing** to other words. When a word ends with one vowel followed by one consonant, double the consonant before adding **-ed** or **-ing.**

Read the words and add **-ed** and **-ing** to each one. Write the new words in the blanks.

		Add **-ed**	Add **-ing**
1.	mail	*mailed* _____	_____
2.	hop	_____	_____
3.	plant	_____	_____
4.	talk	_____	_____
5.	chip	_____	_____

Read the list of words below. Then read each sentence that follows. Add **-ed** or **-ing** to one of the list words to complete each sentence. Write the word in the blank. The word you form must make sense in the sentence.

thank   ask   bag   stop   sweep

1. Star _____*asked*_____ me to help her with some yard work.

2. We began by _____ the leaves into piles.

3. Then we _____ the leaves.

4. Star and I _____ when it became too dark to work.

5. Star's dad _____ me for my help.

Endings: -ED and -ING

Name _____

Many new words can be formed by adding **-ed** or **-ing** to other words. When a word ends in **e,** drop the **e** before adding **-ed** or **-ing.** When a word ends in a consonant followed by **y,** change **y** to **i** before adding **-ed.** Do not change **y** to **i** before adding **-ing** to a word that ends in **y.**

save   sav**ing**
hurry hurr**ied**
carry carry**ing**

Read the words and add **-ed** and **-ing** to each one. Write the new words in the blanks.

		Add **-ed**	Add **-ing**
1.	taste	*tasted*	_____
2.	cry	_____	_____
3.	wave	_____	_____
4.	hope	_____	_____
5.	marry	_____	_____

Read the list of words below. Then read each sentence that follows. Add **-ed** or **-ing** to one of the list words to complete each sentence. Write the word in the blank. The word you form must make sense in the sentence.

shine   try   race   carry   skate

1. Yoko hit the ball and ___*raced*___ toward first base.

2. My friends _____ to play softball in the rain.

3. The dog is _____ a stick in its mouth.

4. Have you ever _____ on that frozen pond?

5. I can't see because the light is _____ in my eyes.

Adding -ed and -ing to verbs in isolation and in context

Endings: -S and -ES

Name _____

Often new words can be formed by adding **-s** or **-es** to other words. To change many words, add the letter **-s.** When a word ends in a consonant followed by **y,** change the **y** to **i** and add **-es.**

laugh	laugh**s**
marry	marr**ies**

Read the words and add **-s** or **-es** to each one. Write the new words in the blanks.

1. draw   _draws_

2. copy   _____

3. study   _____

4. sing   _____

5. walk   _____

6. hurry   _____

Read the list of words below. Then read each sentence that follows. Add **-s** or **-es** to one of the list words to complete each sentence. The word you form must make sense in the sentence.

listen   need   like   try   help   study   make

1. My friend Marcos _____likes_____ to keep busy.

2. Before Marcos goes to school, he _____ his lunch for the next day.

3. He _____ carefully to his teacher.

4. After school he _____ young children learn to swim.

5. Marcos _____ his best to get to all of his little sister's baseball games.

6. When he gets home, Marcos does his homework and _____ for his tests.

7. I think Marcos _____ much longer days.

Endings: -ES

Name _____

bus	bus**es**	pitch	pitch**es**
miss	miss**es**	mix	mix**es**
fish	fish**es**		

Many new words can be formed by adding **-es** to other words. When a word ends in **s, ss, sh, ch,** or **x,** add **-es.**

Read the words. Underline the **s, ss, sh, ch,** or **x** if it comes at the end of a word. Then add **-es** to these words. Write the new words in the blanks.

1. coach   _coaches_

2. reach   _____

3. push   _____

4. pass   _____

5. dress   _____

6. wax   _____

Read the sentences and the list of words. Add **-es** to one of the list words to complete each sentence. Write the word in the blank. The word you form must make sense in the sentence.

1. After school each child _dresses_ in play clothes.

2. Everyone _____ to Mrs. Bello's backyard.

3. The scout leader _____ children about camping.

4. James _____ his test when he ties the knots.

5. He _____ that he could spend the night at the lake.

6. Alma _____ the dirt from her backpack.

7. She pitches a tent while Tony _____ every step.

8. Using the campfire, Lin _____ a snack.

teach
dress
rush
watch
pass
fix
wish
brush

Adding -es to verbs in isolation and in context

Base Words and Endings

Name _____

A word to which an ending can be added is called a base word. | **reach**es

Read each word and write its base word in the blank.

1. closing _____close_____
2. knowing _____
3. skipped _____
4. batting _____
5. standing _____
6. makes _____

7. dried _____
8. skating _____
9. stepped _____
10. misses _____
11. tasted _____
12. copies _____

Read the list of base words below. Then read each sentence that follows. Complete the sentence by adding the ending shown beside the sentence to a word from the list. Write the new word in the blank.

bake   talk   try   run   find   fish

1. One day we were _____talking_____ about ways that we have fun.   -ing

2. Andrew told us he _____ in a pond near his home.   -es

3. Molly said she _____ seashells on the beach.   -s

4. Jim _____ to explain a guessing game he likes.   -ed

5. Allen said he likes _____ in a race more than anything else.   -ing

6. Jessie told how she had a lot of fun when she _____ bread for her friends.   -ed

Endings: -ER and -EST

Name _____

In many words, the ending **-er** means "more." It can be used to compare two things. The ending **-est** means "most." It can be used to compare three or more things.	deep deep**er** deep deep**est**

Read the sentences and the word choices. Circle the word that makes sense in each sentence.

1. This year's dog show should be (greater, greatest) than last year's show.

2. There will be a race to see which of the many dogs can run (faster, fastest).

3. Seth hopes that his dog is (quicker, quickest) than his cousin's dog.

4. A prize will be given to the (smaller, smallest) of all the dogs.

5. The (younger, youngest) dog of all might be one of Spot's puppies.

6. My dog may be the (older, oldest) dog there, but she is also the best dog in the show!

Read each sentence and the word beside it. Add **-er** or **-est** to the word to complete the sentence. Write the new word in the blank. The word you form must make sense in the sentence.

1. I must be the _____*slowest*_____ shopper in this town.   slow

2. To save money, I try to find the _____ of all the prices.   low

3. Because I am _____ than I was last year, I must buy some new clothes.   tall

4. My dad says I might have to buy the _____ priced pants in the store.   high

5. I guess I take a _____ time choosing my things than you do.   long

Using -er or -est for comparison; Adding -er or -est to adjectives and adverbs in context

Endings: -ER and -EST

Name _____

Many new words can be formed by adding **-er** or **-est** to other words. When a word ends with one vowel followed by one consonant, double the consonant before adding **-er** or **-est**. When a word ends in **e**, drop the **e** before adding **-er** or **-est**. When a word ends in a consonant followed by **y,** change the **y** to **i** before adding **-er** or **-est**.

wet	wett**est**
wise	wis**er**
cloudy	cloud**ier**

Add **-er** and **-est** to each word below. Write the new words in the blanks.

		Add **-er**	Add **-est**
1.	busy	*busier*	_____
2.	big	_____	_____
3.	sunny	_____	_____
4.	late	_____	_____
5.	light	_____	_____

Read each sentence and the word beside it. Add **-er** or **-est** to the word to complete the sentence. Write the new word in the blank. The word you form must make sense in the sentence.

1. Lance's shop has the _____*cutest*_____ stuffed toys I've seen.   cute

2. The orange cat is _____ than my yellow cat.   fat

3. That clown has the _____ hat that I've seen.   funny

4. You'd like seeing the deer that is _____ than a person.   tall

5. The shop has the _____ toys of any store in town.   fine

Adding -er and -est to adjectives in isolation and in context

Endings: -ER and -EST

Name _____

Read each sentence and the word shown below the blank. Add **-er** or **-est** to the word to complete the sentence. Write the new word in the blank.

1. This book is _____*sillier*_____ than the book about the pink turtle.
    (silly)

2. Will the stove get _____ than it is now?
    (hot)

3. Can you make this room look _____ than it looked before?
    (neat)

4. Please buy the _____ poster you can find.
    (bright)

5. Is that the _____ of all the hot-air balloons in the show?
    (big)

6. Where can I buy the _____ flowers in town?
    (nice)

7. The day of the school play is our _____ day of the year.
    (busy)

8. This metal ring is _____ than the wooden ring I used to have.
    (loose)

9. Ellen's apartment is _____ to the school than mine is.
    (close)

10. The baby looked _____ after she took her nap.
    (happy)

11. Brenda's dog is _____ than Ken's dog.
    (fat)

Adding -er or -est to adjectives in context

Endings

Name _____

Read the list of words below. Then read each sentence that follows. Complete the sentence by adding one of the endings shown beside the sentence to a word from the list. Write the new word in the blank. The word you form must make sense in the sentence.

fish	bat	chase	study	jump	bake

1. Tim's father _____*bakes*_____ bread in the new oven.   -s, -es

2. Peggy _____ for trout in a stream near the park.   -s, -es

3. Will you be _____ in the next baseball game?   -ed, -ing

4. Len _____ his spelling words each morning.   -es, -ing

5. Elena _____ into the swimming pool from the diving board.   -ed, -ing

6. Today I _____ my kitten around the house.   -ed, -ing

Add **-er** and **-est** to each word below. Write the new words in the blanks.

	Add **-er**	Add **-est**
1. slow	*slower*	_____
2. sad	_____	_____
3. fine	_____	_____
4. pretty	_____	_____
5. large	_____	_____
6. loud	_____	_____

Review of adding -ed, -ing, -s, or -es to verbs in context; Adding -er and -est to adjectives

Plurals: -S and -ES

<u>Name</u> _____

A word that stands for one of something is a singular word. A word that stands for two or more of something is a plural word. To write the plural form of most words, add **-s.** To form the plural of a word that ends in **s, ss, sh, ch,** or **x,** add **-es.** To form the plural of a word that ends in a consonant followed by **y,** change the **y** to **i** and add **-es.**

toy	toy**s**
lunch	lunch**es**
baby	bab**ies**

Read the words. Write the plural form of each one.

1. shoe _____*shoes*_____

2. watch _____

3. brush _____

4. party _____

5. boss _____

6. room _____

7. puppy _____

8. fox _____

Read the sentences and the list of words. Write the plural form of a word from the list to complete each sentence. The word you form must make sense in the sentence.

1. We can ride our _____*bikes*_____ to the market.

2. Let's go after we eat and do the _____.

3. Eva wants us to buy some _____ that can be planted.

4. She will plant them in the ground in straight _____.

5. We can pay for the flowers with five dollars and some

   _____.

6. We will ask for _____ to hold the daisies we buy.

row

box

dish

six

bike

penny

daisy

story

Forming plurals in isolation and in context: -s and es

Plurals: Changing F to V

Name _____

To write the plural form of most words that end in **f** or **fe**, change the **f** or **fe** to **v** and add **-es**.

leaf	lea**ves**
life	li**ves**

Read each sentence and the words beside it. Write the plural form of one of the words to complete each sentence. The word you form must make sense in the sentence.

1. The cook uses sharp _knives_ to cut the meat.

   life
   knife

2. How many _____ of bread are needed to make forty sandwiches?

   loaf
   leaf

3. In this make-believe story, a group of _____ makes a family very happy.

   shelf
   elf

4. Most of those _____ were born last week.

   calf
   half

5. The tree grows new _____ each spring.

   leaf
   life

6. This book tells about the _____ of well-known men and women.

   life
   loaf

7. In the play, a bank was robbed by two _____.

   thief
   knife

8. My brother and sister learned how to build _____ for their books.

   shelf
   self

Irregular Plurals

Name _____

The plurals of some words are formed by changing the spelling of their singular forms.

child - children	man - men	woman - women
tooth - teeth	foot - feet	mouse - mice
goose - geese		

The plural forms of some words can be the same as their singular forms.

sheep   deer   fish

Read each set of sentences and its list of words. Write the plural form of a word from the list to complete each sentence. The word you form must make sense in the sentence.

1. *Children* ___ will enjoy seeing the puppet show.

2. How much wool can you get from six _____?

3. I have seen _____ flying over our campsite.

4. Many women and _____ will vote tomorrow.

5. I found a nest of baby _____ that were each smaller than my thumb.

man
fish
Child
foot
goose
sheep
mouse

1. Every morning, Dad asks me if I have brushed my _____.

2. We need more men and _____ to drive the school buses.

3. If we wait near the woods, we might see some _____.

4. The new shoes I am wearing make my _____ hurt.

5. Joy came home carrying a pail filled with _____ that she caught at the lake.

fish
woman
deer
tooth
child
foot
mouse

Forming irregular plurals in context

Plurals

Name _____

Read the paragraphs and the list of words. Write the plural form of a word from the list to complete each sentence. The words you form must make sense in the paragraph.

I think you will like this store better than the ___*stores*___

we shopped in before. It is full of things for _____ under

the age of twelve. The clothing part of the store has jeans, shirts, and

_____. Another part of the store has _____

to tell time, as well as rings and bracelets.

Most children like to look at the toys. They are in the biggest part of

the store. The _____ are full of every kind of toy. There

are dolls that look like newborn _____, and dolls that are

dressed like grown men and _____. I have seen sets of

_____ you could eat from and small sinks and stoves.

There are also toy foods, such as apples and _____.

You might like seeing the stuffed animals like those puppies and

_____. I never leave the store without looking at the

_____ that can be played by one or more players. You

can see why I save my _____ before I visit this store!

watch

baby

calf

store

peach

shelf

dress

dish

penny

child

game

woman

Showing Ownership

<u>Name</u> _____

To make most words show ownership, add an apostrophe (') and **s.** In the example, **dog's bone,** the **'s** shows that the bone belongs to the dog.

dog's bone

Rewrite each group of words below, adding **'s** to form words that show ownership.

1. the horse that Bruce owns   *Bruce's horse* _____

2. the sock that the baby wears   _____

3. the windows of a truck   _____

4. the backpack that Sal owns   _____

5. the game that belongs to Kim   _____

6. the paw of a cat   _____

Read each sentence and the words beside it. Add **'s** to one of the words to complete the sentence. The word you form must make sense in the sentence.

1. The _____*bank's*_____ doors open each day at nine o'clock.   bank / book

2. My _____ office is in the center of the town.   apple / aunt

3. Her _____ speech was heard by many people.   father / farm

4. The _____ flowers are light pink.   brush / bush

5. My math _____ writing is easy to read.   teacher / tractor

Forming singular possessives in isolation and in context

Showing Ownership

Name _____

To make a singular word show ownership, add an apostrophe (') and **s**. To make a plural word that ends in **s** show ownership, add just an apostrophe. In the examples, **'s** shows that the bones belong to one dog, and **s'** shows that the bones belong to more than one dog.

dog's bones
dogs' bones

Read the words and look at the pictures. Circle the words that tell about each picture.

girl's gloves (girls' gloves)	tree's bark trees' bark	truck's wheels trucks' wheels
dog's food dogs' food	boy's photos boys' photos	skunk's stripes skunks' stripes

Rewrite each group of words below, adding **'** or **'s** to the underlined word to show ownership.

1. the wings of the <u>birds</u>   *birds' wings*

2. the tent that is used by the <u>scouts</u>   _____

3. the house that belongs to a <u>teacher</u>   _____

4. the office used by two <u>dentists</u>   _____

5. the covers of the <u>books</u>   _____

6. the tail of a <u>monkey</u>   _____

Recognize meanings of singular and plural possessives; Forming singular and plural possessives

Showing Ownership

Name _____

Read each sentence and the words shown below the blank. Write the word that makes sense in the sentence.

1. The _____*dog's*_____ tail is short and brown.
   (dog's, dogs')

2. The two _____ steering wheels are the same color.
   (truck's, trucks')

3. That _____ stripes are green and white.
   (flag's, flags')

4. The _____ birthdays are on the same day.
   (boy's, boys')

5. Did you see _____ new puppy?
   (Marys', Mary's)

6. I could see the _____ heads through the little window.
   (cat's, cats')

7. My youngest _____ blocks are on her bedroom floor.
   (sister's, sisters')

8. We found _____ hammer under the steps.
   (Mother's, Mothers')

9. The _____ coat is always kept clean.
   (kittens', kitten's)

10. The _____ floors are made of wood.
    (room's, rooms')

11. My _____ nose was sunburned yesterday.
    (friend's, friends')

12. The _____ engines were made in this city.
    (car's, cars')

Using singular and plural possessives in context

Plurals and Showing Ownership

Name _____

Read the words and write the plural form of each one.

1. bicycle *bicycles*

8. party _____

2. wolf _____

9. glass _____

3. school _____

10. man _____

4. baby _____

11. patch _____

5. child _____

12. deer _____

6. box _____

13. elf _____

7. apple _____

14. puppy _____

Rewrite each group of words below, adding **'** or **'s** to the underlined word to show ownership.

1. the whiskers of the <u>cats</u>   *cats' whiskers*

2. the field that is used by the <u>players</u> _____

3. the apartment that belongs to <u>Joan</u> _____

4. the library used by the <u>teachers</u> _____

5. the playground owned by the <u>school</u> _____

6. the hats worn by the <u>fire fighters</u> _____

7. the smile of the <u>child</u> _____

8. the backpack that belongs to <u>Bob</u> _____

Endings and Plurals

Name _____

Read each sentence and the word beside it. Complete each sentence by adding one of the endings shown below to the word. Write the new word in the blank. The word you form must make sense in the sentence.

-ed   -ing   -s   -es   -er   -est

1. A storm began while we were _playing_ in the yard.   play

2. That is the _____ hat I have ever seen!   silly

3. A few of us _____ the logs for the fire.   carry

4. Aunt Janet _____ me every time I visit.   thank

5. When Dave's football clothes are dirty, he _____ them.   wash

6. The crowd _____ when the show was over.   clap

7. Celina seems _____ today than she was yesterday.   happy

8. Every afternoon a jet _____ over our house.   fly

Read the words and write the plural form of each one.

1. brush   _brushes_   7. mouse   _____

2. friend   _____   8. city   _____

3. box   _____   9. match   _____

4. book   _____   10. shelf   _____

5. buggy   _____   11. sheep   _____

6. knife   _____   12. class   _____

Assessment of adding endings to base words in context; Forming plurals

Showing Ownership

Name _____

Read each sentence and the words beside it. Write the word that makes sense in each sentence.

1. This spelling _____*book's*_____ pages are ripped.   book's
books'

2. Her _____ bedrooms are painted red and blue.   brother's
brothers'

3. Our many _____ leaves are different shades of green.   tree's
trees'

4. _____ school was built last year.   Jack's
Jacks'

5. The three _____ noses were shiny and red.   clown's
clowns'

6. The bedroom _____ ring woke me up.   phone's
phones'

7. The _____ lawn is always green.   park's
parks'

8. All of these _____ frames are made of wood and metal.   picture's
pictures'

9. The _____ trunks are strong enough to carry logs.   elephant's
elephants'

10. My oldest _____ shoe size is a five.   sister's
sisters'

Assessment of using singular and plural possessives in context

Name _____

The Boy Who Cried "Wolf!"

This is a story that teaches something important about life. Read to see if you can find out what it is.

Once there was a boy who looked after sheep. He had nothing to do all day but watch the sheep, and he was bored.

One day the boy thought of a way to have some fun, so he ran into the village shouting, "Wolf! Wolf! A wolf is after the sheep!"

All the people in the village left their work to help the boy. But when they reached the place where the sheep were grazing, there was no wolf in sight. The boy laughed at the people for believing his trick. The next day the boy played the same trick. Now he was having fun.

On the third day, the boy saw a hungry wolf coming near the flock, and he got very frightened. He ran as fast as his legs would carry him to the village. "Help!" he cried. "A wolf is going to kill the sheep!"

But this time the people did not leave their work to help the boy. They said, "That boy is just trying to fool us again by telling another lie." When the boy returned to the sheep, he saw that the wolf had killed them all.

The people were very angry when they found out the boy had not been telling a lie this time. They said, "People who tell lies cannot be believed even when they say something that is true."

A. Answer the following questions.
 1. What was the job of the boy in the story?

 _____

 2. Why did the boy play a trick?

 _____

 3. What did the people do the first time the boy played his trick?

 _____

Application of reading and comprehension skills in a literature context

Name _____

B. Check the two words in each line that have the same meaning in the story.

1. _____ play   _____ fool   _____ trick

2. _____ flock   _____ sheep   _____ grazing

C. Answer the following questions.
   1. What does this story teach about life?

   _____

   _____

   2. Do you think the people were right or wrong not to believe the boy the third time he cried, "Wolf"? Tell why or why not.

   _____

   _____

D. Write a story about one of the following sayings.

   If you want something to be done right, do it yourself.
   In time of trouble, you find out who your true friends are.
   Those who harm others often end up harming themselves.

   _____

   _____

   _____

   _____

   _____

Application of thinking and writing skills in a literature context

Compound Words

Name _____

A compound word is formed by joining two smaller words together.

dog + house = doghouse

Read each compound word and write the two words that form it.

1. waterfall _____water_____ _____fall_____

2. snowflakes _____ _____

3. grandson _____ _____

4. bookcase _____ _____

5. doorbell _____ _____

6. rainstorm _____ _____

7. lighthouse _____ _____

Read the sentences. Circle the two compound words in each sentence.

1. Can you use your (snowplow) on our (driveway)?

2. I found a starfish and a few seashells on the beach.

3. Jean will fold the bedspread that goes in her bedroom.

4. My grandfather makes homemade bean soup.

5. I must have left my raincoat on the playground.

6. Have you ever watched a sunset from the tall building downtown?

7. The plants will not grow without sunshine.

Identifying words that form compound words; Identifying compound words in context

Compound Words

Name _____

Read the words in each list below. Draw lines to match the words that form compound words.

book	place	side	noon
rain	fall	snow	paper
pan	day	after	walk
fire	case	fire	storm
birth	cakes	news	wood

Read the list of words below. Then read the sentences that follow. Write the word from the list that makes sense in each sentence.

notebook   cookbook   sometimes   something   oatmeal
airplane   rowboat   grandmother   airport

1. I plan to write to my *grandmother*, who lives in New York.

2. She will enjoy reading about my _____ ride on the lake.

3. She may remember the time we went to the city _____.

4. We flew in an _____ that took us over the town.

5. We did that because Grandmother wanted me to try

    _____ new.

6. She _____ wants me to taste something I've never
    eaten before.

7. Once she tried to make me eat _____.

8. As a joke, I bought her a new _____ to read.

9. I could fill a _____ with stories about Grandmother and me!

Forming compound words; Using compound words in context

Compound Words

Name _____

Read the sentences below. Use two words from each sentence to form a compound word. Write the compound word in the blank.

1. A bird that is blue is called a ___*bluebird*___.

2. A walk near the side of a road is a _____.

3. A cloth that covers a table is a _____.

4. The bud of a rose is a _____.

5. A ball that is thrown through a basket is a _____.

6. A brush that is used to clean each tooth is a _____.

7. Work that is done for school is called _____.

8. A shell that can be found near the sea is a _____.

9. Corn that you can pop is called _____.

10. A bell that is near the door of a house is a _____.

11. A pot that holds tea is a _____.

12. Wood that is used to build a fire is called _____.

13. The print of a foot made in sand is called a _____.

14. Work done at home is _____.

15. A tub for a bath is a _____.

16. A boat that has a sail is a _____.

Forming compound words in context

Contractions

Name _____

A contraction is a short way to write two words. It is written by putting two words together and leaving out a letter or letters. An apostrophe (') takes the place of the letters that are left out. The word **won't** is a special contraction made from the words **will** and **not.**

is + not = **isn't**
will + not = **won't**
we + are = **we're**
I + will = **I'll**

Read the list of contractions below. Then read the pairs of words that follow. Write a contraction from the list that stands for each word pair.

| it's | she'll | weren't |
| we'd | hadn't | they're |

1. had not   *hadn't*   4. she will   _____

2. were not _____   5. we would _____

3. they are _____   6. it is   _____

Read each sentence and the pair of words shown below the blank. Complete the sentence by writing the contraction that stands for the word pair.

1. Does he know that _____*we're*_____ coming home early?
    (we are)

2. Tammy _____ find the letter she wrote.
    (could not)

3. John _____ ready to swim in the deep end of the pool.
    (was not)

4. We _____ go to school in the summer.
    (do not)

5. Did you know that _____ been visiting their friends?
    (they have)

6. Ellen _____ be able to come to our party.
    (will not)

Forming contractions in isolation and in context

123

Contractions

Read the contractions below. Then write the two words for which each contraction stands.

1. wouldn't   *would not*   6. he'll   _____

2. we've   _____   7. hasn't   _____

3. didn't   _____   8. she's   _____

4. that's   _____   9. won't   _____

5. we'd   _____   10. I've   _____

Read each sentence and the contraction shown below the blank. Complete the sentence by writing the two words for which the contraction stands.

1. *I would* _____ like to move to a warmer part of the country.
    (I'd)

2. It _____ snow where you live, does it?
    (doesn't)

3. _____ not seen a snowflake since you moved there.
    (You've)

4. I _____ be able to go sled riding if I lived where you live.
    (wouldn't)

5. _____ not cold enough to go ice skating, either.
    (It's)

6. _____ not sure I want to move after all.
    (I'm)

Identifying words that form contractions in isolation and in context

Contractions

Name _____

Read each sentence and find the two words in it that can be made into a contraction. Circle the two words and write the contraction in the blank.

1. The city zoo (was not) far from our school building.

   wasn't

2. It did not take the bus driver long to get there.

   _____

3. Kelly and Ross could not wait to see the animals.

   _____

4. They had been counting the days until the trip.

   _____

5. Kelly says that she is going to work in a zoo someday.

   _____

Read the sentences and the list of contractions. Write the contraction that makes sense in each sentence. The word you write must make sense in the sentence.

1. _Shouldn't_ Amy read the story to the class?

2. Jordan and Juan _____ here when she read it before.

3. I think _____ be sorry they missed the funny ending.

4. I told Ms. Mendes that we _____ made the story into a play.

5. She told us _____ what had been planned.

6. We can start planning after _____ heard the story.

they'll
that's
won't
didn't
Shouldn't
we've
weren't
should've

Forming contractions in context; Using contractions in context

Compound Words and Contractions

Name _____

Read the clues below. Use two words from each clue to form a compound word. Write the compound word in the blank.

1. a coat worn in the rain   _raincoat_

2. a boat that you can row   _____

3. a tie that is worn around the neck   _____

4. work done around the house   _____

5. a book that tells you how to cook   _____

6. water from a stream that falls over a high place   _____

7. a bell that is rung at the door of a home   _____

Read the word pairs below. Then write the contraction that stands for each word pair.

1. we are   _we're_   8. have not   _____

2. will not   _____   9. they have   _____

3. he will   _____   10. can not   _____

4. you would   _____   11. I am   _____

5. are not   _____   12. she had   _____

6. they are   _____   13. do not   _____

7. we have   _____   14. there is   _____

Review of forming compound words; Forming contractions

Compound Words and Contractions

Name _____

Read the list of words below. Then read the sentences that follow. Choose a word from the list to complete the compound word in each sentence. The compound word you form must make sense in the sentence.

place	port	work
case	way	room

1. I read my book and finished my home_work_.

2. Each of my books is now in the book_____.

3. I took my bath and cleaned the tub in the bath_____.

4. I helped my mom build a fire in the fire_____.

5. Soon, Dad will bring my uncle home from the air_____.

6. I can't wait until I see them pull into the drive_____.

Read each sentence and the pair of words beside it. Complete each sentence with a contraction that stands for the word pair.

1. _____I'll_____ show you how to make paper airplanes.   I will

2. _____ not as hard to make as you may think.   They are

3. _____ the pattern for the plane you want to make?   Where is

4. I think _____ enjoy using this colored paper.   you would

5. We _____ tried folding the heavier white paper.   have not

6. _____ we start with the smallest plane?   Should not

Prefixes: UN- and DIS-

Name _____

A prefix is a letter or group of letters that can be added to the beginning of a word. The prefixes **un-** and **dis-** mean "not" or "the opposite of." For example, the word **unlock** means "the opposite of lock." The word **dislike** means "not like."

un + lock = **un**lock
dis + like = **dis**like

Read the list of words below. Then read each sentence that follows. Add **un-** to one of the list words to complete each sentence. Write the new word in the blank. The word you form must make sense in the sentence.

safe	load	happy	lock

1. We need help to _____*unload*_____ the logs from the truck.

2. The busy street is _____ for the children who walk to school.

3. The small child looked _____ when she let go of her balloon.

4. You will need a key to _____ the front door.

Read the list of words below. Then read each sentence that follows. Add **dis-** to one of the list words to complete each sentence. Write the new word in the blank. The word you form must make sense in the sentence.

cover	connect	agree	liked	color

1. The bright light of the sun may _____*discolor*_____ the camper's tent.

2. The scientists hope to _____ a cure for the illness.

3. Joey _____ singing in the class play.

4. Ms. Miller will _____ the wire before she fixes the lamp.

5. Because we _____, we should talk about the problem.

Forming words with prefixes *un-* and *dis-*; Words containing prefixes in context

Prefixes: RE- and PRE-

Name _____

The prefix **re-** means "again." For example, the word **refill** means "fill again." The prefix **pre-** means "before." The word **prepay** means "pay before."	**re** + fill = **re**fill **pre** + pay = **pre**pay

Read the clues. Add **re-** or **pre-** to the underlined base word to form a word that matches the clue.

1. to <u>wrap</u> again   *rewrap*

2. to <u>test</u> before   _____

3. to <u>write</u> again   _____

4. to <u>paint</u> again   _____

5. to <u>use</u> again   _____

6. before a <u>game</u>   _____

Read each sentence and the words beside it. Write the word that makes sense in each sentence.

1.	Ardis brought a book home from her *preschool* class.	retell preschool pregame
2.	Do you know how to _____ the part on the bike?	reread replay replace
3.	The bill was _____ a week ago.	prepaid pregame replayed
4.	We watched the band march in the _____ show.	retell prepaid pregame
5.	Are you able to _____ the tale you heard last night?	reread retell preheat
6.	Please _____ the story for the class.	replace replay reread

Prefixes: OVER- and MIS-

Name _____

The prefix **over-** means "too much." For example, the word **overdo** means "to do too much." The prefix **mis-** means "badly" or "wrongly." For example, the word **misuse** means "to use wrongly."

over + do = **over**do
mis + use = **mis**use

Read the list of words below. Then read each sentence that follows. Add **over-** to one of the list words to complete each sentence. Write the new word in the blank. The word you form must make sense in the sentence.

eat   sleep   cook   load   flow

1. Did you ___*oversleep*___ on the first day of school?

2. Be careful not to _____ your book bag.

3. The rain made the river _____.

4. The good food made me want to _____.

5. If you _____ the meat, it will be dry.

Read the list of words below. Then read each sentence that follows. Add **mis-** to one of the list words to complete each sentence. Write the new word in the blank. The word you form must make sense in the sentence.

understand   spell   place   treat   lead

1. If you ___*mistreat*___ your bike, it will not run well.

2. When you _____ a word, cross it out and write it correctly.

3. Did you _____ what needed to be done?

4. If you _____ your homework, you must find it or redo it.

5. That sign will _____ travelers.

Forming words with prefixes *over-* and *mis-*; Words containing prefixes in context

Prefixes

Name _____

Read each sentence and the word beside it. Add **un-, pre-,** or **over-** to the word to complete each sentence. Write the new word in the blank. The word you form must make sense in the sentence.

1. The _____*unfair*_____ rules were changed.   fair

2. I _____ the cost at the time I ordered.   paid

3. If you don't wake her, she will _____.   sleep

4. My dog _____ when there is too much food in the dish.   eats

5. Because I lost the game, I felt _____.   lucky

6. Scott talks about his _____ class.   school

Read each sentence and the word beside it. Add **dis-, re-,** or **mis-** to the word to complete each sentence. Write the new word in the blank. The word you form must make sense in the sentence.

1. If you _____*disagree*_____ with me, let me know.   agree

2. Grandma will _____ many of her stories.   tell

3. I often _____ the time when I get busy.   judge

4. I will _____ the chicken soup for lunch.   heat

5. We saw the rabbit _____ from sight into the red hat.   appear

6. If you _____ the sign, you will get lost.   read

Suffixes: -FUL and -LESS

Name _____

A suffix is a letter or group of letters that can be added to the end of a word. The suffix **-ful** usually means "full of." For example, the word **helpful** means "full of help." The suffix **-less** usually means "without." The word **hopeless** means "without hope."

help + **ful** = help**ful**
hope + **less** = hope**less**

Read the words below. Form new words by adding the suffix **-ful** or **-less** to the words. Write each word under the correct heading.

end	hand	wonder	friend	play	cloud	forget	home

Add **-ful**	Add **-less**
handful	_____
_____	_____
_____	_____
_____	_____

Read the sentences and the list of words. Write the word from the list that makes sense in each sentence.

1. I was _____*careless*_____ when I lost my math paper.

2. Put a small _____ of salt into the soup.

3. I slept well and had a _____ night.

4. We are _____ that we have friends like you.

5. I am glad the snake we saw is _____.

6. The list of jobs to do at home seems _____.

careless
restful
helpful
harmless
sleepless
thankful
spoonful
endless

Forming words with suffixes -ful and -less; Words containing suffixes in context

Suffixes: -Y and -LY

Name _____

The suffixes **-y** and **-ly** can be added to some words. For example, a day with **rain** is a **rainy** day. Something done in a **nice** way is done **nicely**.

rain + **y** = rain**y**
nice + **ly** = nice**ly**

Read the list of words below. Then read each sentence that follows. Add **-y** to one of the list words to complete each sentence. Write the new word in the blank. The word you form must make sense in the sentence.

frost   cloud   stick   luck   squeak

1. We were _____*lucky*_____ to get five tickets for the early show last Saturday.

2. I spilled some glue, and my desk is now _____.

3. We didn't see much sunshine because the sky was _____.

4. My new boots make a _____ sound when I walk.

5. Because it is cold outdoors, our windows look white and _____.

Read the list of words below. Then read each sentence that follows. Add **-ly** to one of the list words to complete each sentence. Write the new word in the blank. The word you form must make sense in the sentence.

soft   week   quick   friend   slow

1. Because he walked _____*slowly*_____, he missed the bus.

2. If we get dressed _____, we can go sled riding before we eat.

3. My older brother reads a _____ newspaper.

4. She played the song so _____ that we could hardly hear it.

5. We had fun at the party because we met some _____ people.

Forming words with suffixes -y and -ly; Words containing suffixes in context

Suffixes: -ABLE and -ISH

Name _____

The suffix **-able** means "can be" or "able to be." For example, the word **washable** means "can be washed." The suffix **-ish** means "like" or "somewhat." The word **childish** means "like a child."

wash + **able** = wash**able**
child + **ish** = child**ish**

Read the words below. Form new words by adding the suffix **-able** or **-ish** to the words. Write each word under the correct heading.

yellow   baby   break   pass   girl   like   clown   change

Add **-able**	Add **-ish**
breakable	_____
_____	_____
_____	_____
_____	_____

Read the sentences and the list of words. Add **-able** or **-ish** to one of the list words to complete each sentence. Write the word in the blank. The word you form must make sense in the sentence.

1. The low shelf makes the toys _*reachable*_.

2. The pond's water looks _____.

3. It is _____ to cross the street without looking both ways.

4. That page got wet, so the words are no longer _____.

5. You can get the stain out of a _____ shirt.

wash

green

reach

fool

read

Forming words with suffixes -able and -ish: Words containing suffixes in context

Suffixes

Name _____

Read each sentence and the suffixes beside it. Add one of the suffixes to the word shown below the blank to complete the sentence. The word you form must make sense in the sentence.

1. Please speak ___*loudly*___ when you give your speech.
    (loud)

    -ful
    -ly

2. Berta has brown eyes and long, _____ brown hair.
    (curl)

    -y
    -ful

3. After looking for my bike for an hour, I felt _____.
    (hope)

    -less
    -ly

4. Pedro's _____ act was really funny.
    (clown)

    -ly
    -ish

5. The sun was shining, and the sky was _____.
    (cloud)

    -less
    -ful

6. I can help you put some oil on this _____ door.
    (squeak)

    -y
    -ly

7. The children watching the puppet show looked _____.
    (cheer)

    -ish
    -ful

8. Billy is _____ to all of his team members.
    (friend)

    -ly
    -able

9. I will be _____ and tell you how I feel.
    (truth)

    -ful
    -less

10. Marta's new sweater is _____.
    (wash)

    -less
    -able

Forming words with suffixes in context: *-ful, -less, -y, -ly, -able, -ish*

Read the clues. Add one of the prefixes or suffixes from the list to each underlined base word to form a word that matches the clue.

1. full of <u>truth</u>   *truthful*

2. having <u>frost</u>   _____

3. the opposite of <u>agree</u>   _____

4. to <u>write</u> again   _____

5. the opposite of <u>trust</u>   _____

6. to <u>pay</u> before   _____

7. without <u>pain</u>   _____

8. full of <u>care</u>   _____

pre-

dis-

re-

-ful

-less

-y

---

1. to <u>do</u> too much   _____

2. not <u>true</u>   _____

3. like a <u>child</u>   _____

4. <u>read</u> wrongly   _____

5. every <u>week</u>   _____

6. able to <u>change</u>   _____

7. to <u>sleep</u> too much   _____

8. not <u>hurt</u>   _____

un-

over-

mis-

-ly

-able

-ish

Review of forming words with prefixes and suffixes

Prefixes and Suffixes

Name _____

Read the list of words below. Circle the prefix or suffix in each word.

thought(ful)	thankless	readable	mistreat
greenish	disconnect	fairly	unsafe
overflow	replace	preheat	rusty

Read the list of words below. Then read the sentences that follow. Write the word from the list that makes sense in each sentence.

| unpack | helpless | disappear | rewrap | restful | misplace |
| rocky | overload | pregame | neatly | grayish | breakable |

1. The book about magic tricks shows you how to make a ball _disappear_.

2. There will be a _____ show on the football field.

3. When Bill gets home, he will _____ his suitcases.

4. Please _____ the leftover food and put it in the freezer.

5. We felt _____ when we couldn't fix the car.

6. Climbing up the _____ hillside took us most of the day.

7. Did you _____ the books you brought home?

8. I will be careful when I wash the _____ vase.

9. My new cat has a _____ coat and white paws.

10. Because I felt ill, I was told to have a _____ day at home.

11. The books and papers are stacked _____ on the shelves.

12. The truck will not run well if you _____ it.

Assessment of identifying prefixes and suffixes; Words containing prefixes and suffixes in context

Syllables

Name _____

Many words are made of small parts called syllables. Because each syllable has one vowel sound, a word has as many syllables as it has vowel sounds. The word **stone** has one vowel sound, so it has one syllable. The word **raincoat** has two vowel sounds, so it has two syllables.

Name the pictures. Write the number of syllables you hear in each picture name.

 _2_

garden

 ___

popcorn

 ___

button

 ___

kitchen

 ___

cage

 ___

ladder

 ___

pineapple

 ___

puppet

 ___

log

 ___

soap

 ___

butterfly

 ___

sixty

Identifying the number of syllables in a word

Syllables

Name _____

A compound word should be divided into syllables between the words that make it compound.

rain/bow

Read the words below. Circle each compound word. Then write each compound word and draw a line between its syllables.

1. (sunset) _sun/set_

2. summer _____

3. someone _____

4. lighthouse _____

5. trouble _____

6. notebook _____

7. highway _____

8. jumping _____

9. broom _____

10. railroad _____

11. starfish _____

12. spray _____

13. doghouse _____

14. baseball _____

15. homemade _____

16. puppy _____

17. without _____

18. bedroom _____

19. teapot _____

20. birthday _____

21. toothbrush _____

22. raindrop _____

23. lifeboat _____

24. sidewalk _____

25. snowflake _____

26. throat _____

27. downtown _____

28. father _____

Identifying and dividing compound words into syllables

Syllables

Name _____

A word that has a prefix or suffix can be divided into syllables between the prefix or suffix and the base word.	un/tie dark/ness

Read the list of words and the sentences. Divide each list word into syllables by drawing a line between the syllables. Then write the word from the list that makes sense in each sentence.

un/tie

pretest

sleepless

thoughtful

refill

dislike

neatly

softly

rewrite

rainy

1. Today I will ___*rewrite*___ my story with a pen.

2. We will _____ the car's gas tank before we start on our trip.

3. Please help me _____ this string so I can open the box.

4. I will sing the song _____ to the baby.

5. Before he started the lesson, the teacher gave us a

   _____ to see what we knew.

6. Calling me on my birthday was a _____ thing for you to do.

7. Because the dog barked for many hours, I had a

   _____ night.

8. I _____ walking to school on rainy days.

9. It is hard to ride a bike on a _____ day.

10. All of the books were _____ placed on the shelves.

Dividing words containing affixes into syllables; Using two-syllable words in context

Syllables

Name _____

When a word has two consonants between two vowels, the word is usually divided between the two consonants.	mon/key cir/cus
	VC/CV VC/CV

Read the list of words. Write each word and draw a line between its syllables.

1. magnet *mag/net*
2. blanket _____
3. harvest _____
4. lumber _____
5. butter _____

6. corner _____
7. mistake _____
8. happen _____
9. basket _____
10. dentist _____

Read each sentence and the words below each blank. Complete each sentence by writing the word that has the VC/CV pattern. Draw a line between its syllables.

1. Last _____*win/ter*_____ we went to see Grandmother and Grandfather.
       (weekend, winter)

2. We can buy food for the picnic at the _____.
                                                (market, store)

3. Did you leave a _____ on my desk this morning?
                        (paper, pencil)

4. The _____ sometimes wears a fancy crown.
           (lady, princess)

5. Place a _____ next to each plate on the table.
                (napkin, fork)

6. The baby held a _____ spoon in her hand.
                        (tiny, silver)

Syllables

Name _____

Words that have one consonant between two vowels can be divided into syllables in two ways. When you see a word that has one consonant between two vowels, say the word. If the first vowel sound is long, divide the word after the first vowel. If the first vowel sound is short, divide the word after the consonant that follows the vowel.

1	ē/ven	pā/per
	V/CV	V/C V
2	vĭs/it	mĕt/al
	VC/V	VC/V

Read the list of words. Write each word. Mark the first vowel of the word with ˘ if it stands for the short sound or ‾ if it stands for the long sound. Then draw a line between its syllables.

1. label   *lā/bel*

2. moment _____

3. cabin _____

4. lemon _____

5. travel _____

6. music _____

7. open _____

8. salad _____

9. robin _____

10. silent _____

11. pupil _____

12. petal _____

13. fever _____

14. planet _____

15. finish _____

16. famous _____

17. siren _____

18. pedal _____

19. tiger _____

20. wagon _____

Dividing words with the V/CV and VC/V patterns into syllables

Syllables

<u>Name</u>

Read the list of words. Write each word and draw a line between its syllables. Mark the first vowel of the word with ˘ if it stands for the short sound or ¯ if it stands for the long sound.

1. camel   *căm/el*

2. acorn   _____

3. palace   _____

4. damage   _____

5. paper   _____

6. closet   _____

7. famous   _____

8. medal   _____

9. bacon   _____

10. minus   _____

Read the list of words and the sentences. Divide each list word into syllables by drawing a line between the syllables. Then write the word from the list that makes sense in each sentence.

h u/m a n

s e c o n d

s h a d o w

f l a v o r

h a b i t

p o n y

p i l o t

s h i v e r

m e t a l

h o t e l

1. I learned how to ride a _*pony*_ when I was young.

2. Greg won _____ prize in the art contest.

3. Our room in the _____ is big enough for the whole family.

4. The _____ can fly the airplane at night.

5. Choose the _____ of ice cream you like best.

6. The shed is made of wood and _____.

7. Packing an apple in my lunch is a _____ for me.

8. Each February we wait to see if the groundhog will see its

_____.

Dividing words with the V/CV and VC/V patterns into syllables; Words containing the V/CV and VC/V patterns in context

143

Syllables

Name _____

Read the words below. Write each word and draw a line between its syllables.

1. chapter   *chap/ter*

2. undress   _____

3. cozy   _____

4. squeaky   _____

5. magic   _____

6. hopeless   _____

7. firewood   _____

8. model   _____

9. picnic   _____

10. truthful   _____

11. button   _____

12. oatmeal   _____

13. closet   _____

14. pretest   _____

15. never   _____

16. minus   _____

17. doorbell   _____

18. notice   _____

19. painless   _____

20. distrust   _____

21. lemon   _____

22. sunny   _____

23. highway   _____

24. later   _____

25. harbor   _____

26. wishbone   _____

27. reuse   _____

28. salad   _____

29. acorn   _____

30. slowly   _____

31. unsafe   _____

32. rewrite   _____

Review of dividing words into syllables

Syllables

Name _____

Read the words below. Write each word and draw a line between its syllables.

1. refill _____re/fill_____

2. friendly _____

3. yellow _____

4. human _____

5. untie _____

6. displease _____

7. pencil _____

8. notebook _____

9. petal _____

10. cheerful _____

Read the list of words and the sentences. Divide each list word into syllables by drawing a line between the syllables. Then write the word from the list that makes sense in each sentence.

t r a v/e l
c l o u d y
s t a r f i s h
b e d r o o m
f a m o u s
n e a t l y
m i s t a k e
u n l o a d
d o c t o r
f i n i s h

1. I visit the _____doctor_____ at least once a year.

2. The team will _____ to the city next weekend.

3. A _____ singer will sing in this show.

4. I made only one _____ on my math test.

5. The _____ sky made us afraid that we wouldn't be able to have our picnic.

6. When I _____ my homework, I can watch the television show.

7. There are two beds in my _____.

8. Please help us _____ the boxes from the truck.

Assessment of dividing words into syllables

Name _____

Safety Rules

Read the following important rules for street safety. Follow these rules yourself and help others follow them, too.

1. Cross streets only at the corners.
2. Always look both ways before you cross the street.
3. Do not cross the street when the light is red.
   Wait until the light turns to green.
4. Do not walk between parked cars.
5. Always walk on the left side of the road, facing the cars.
6. Stop, look, and listen before you cross the railroad tracks.
   Be sure no train is coming.
7. Do not ride your bicycle on the sidewalk.
8. Help little children cross the street safely.
9. Do not get into a car with a stranger.
10. Find a police officer when you see trouble.

A. Finish each rule with the right word or words.

1. Cross only at _____.

2. _____, _____, and _____
   before you cross the railroad tracks.

3. Never get into a car with a _____.

4. Don't ride your bicycle on the _____.

5. Walk on the _____ side of the road, _____
   the cars.

6. When you see trouble, you should find a _____.

7. Before you cross the street, you should look _____ ways.

Application of reading and comprehension skills in a health context

Name _____

B. Finish each idea in your own words.

1. A police officer is someone who _____

_____.

2. A stranger is someone _____.

3. A red light means _____.

4. A green light means _____.

C. Think about these questions. Write answers for two of them.
   Why should you walk on the left side of the road, facing the cars?
   Why shouldn't you walk between parked cars?
   Why should you stop, look, and listen before you cross the railroad tracks?
   Why shouldn't you ride your bicycle on the sidewalk?

1. _____

_____

_____

_____

_____

2. _____

_____

_____

_____

_____

Application of thinking and writing skills in a health context

Antonyms

Name _____

An antonym is a word that has the opposite meaning of another word.	early - late

Read the words in each box below. Draw a line to match each word with its antonym (opposite).

large	old	few	many	slow	hot
young	weak	off	after	cold	fast
strong	small	before	on	over	under

save	bumpy	always	fair	day	night
smooth	spend	unfair	dry	yes	no
early	late	wet	never	frown	smile

Read the list of words below. Then read the sentences that follow. Write the word from the list that is an antonym (opposite) for the underlined word in each sentence.

light	unkind	shut	shout
false	to	down	awake

1. This letter is <u>from</u> Uncle Todd. _____*to*_____

2. I was <u>asleep</u> when Grandfather called. _____

3. Is this living room always so <u>dark</u>? _____

4. Please help me <u>open</u> this heavy door. _____

5. I will <u>whisper</u> the clue to you. _____

6. Is the answer to this question <u>true</u>? _____

7. Please walk <u>up</u> the steps with me. _____

8. Writing that letter was <u>kind</u>. _____

Synonyms

Name _____

| A synonym is a word that has the same or nearly the same meaning as another word. | gift - present |

Read the words in each box below. Draw a line to match each word with its synonym (word that has the same meaning).

talk	sad	hurt	quick	listen	hurry
unhappy	speak	gift	present	rush	hear
small	little	fast	harm	nice	kind

glad	path	big	tell	clean	yell
forest	happy	say	large	breeze	wind
trail	woods	pretty	beautiful	shout	wash

Read the list of words below. Then read the sentences that follow. Write the word from the list that is a synonym (word that has the same meaning) for the underlined word in each sentence.

| nice | cool | run | noisy |
| crowd | strength | sofa | soil |

1. Carmen and Jimmy are sitting on the <u>couch</u>. _____*sofa*_____

2. There was a <u>mob</u> of people in the store. _____

3. Because it is <u>chilly</u> outside, I will wear a sweater. _____

4. Does Kenny have the <u>power</u> to lift that load? _____

5. Would your uncle like to <u>jog</u> with us? _____

6. It was <u>kind</u> of Carly to show me this book. _____

7. I woke up when I heard the <u>loud</u> horn. _____

8. Do you have enough <u>dirt</u> for that plant? _____

Identifying synonyms

Antonyms and Synonyms

Name _____

Read the words below. Circle the two words in each row that are antonyms (opposites).

1.	shiny	(large)	(small)	red	round
2.	fair	happy	little	sad	new
3.	cooked	yes	save	raw	slow
4.	nice	hot	tall	rich	poor
5.	cost	sink	send	float	grow
6.	mix	play	sold	sweet	bought

Read each sentence and the words beside it. Complete each sentence by writing the word that is a synonym (word that has the same meaning) for the word shown below the blank.

1. I will try not to _____*harm*_____ the plants when I walk through the garden. (hurt)

    harm
    water

2. My _____ and I like to eat lunch together. (pals)

    aunt
    friends

3. This map shows where my _____ is. (street)

    road
    home

4. I knew she was happy by the _____ on her face. (grin)

    smile
    look

5. I made a _____ for Timmy's birthday. (present)

    cake
    gift

6. Does Carl know how to _____ a flat tire? (fix)

    remove
    repair

Identifying antonyms and synonyms

Antonyms and Synonyms

Name _____

Read each pair of sentences. In the blanks, write a pair of antonyms (opposites) from the sentences.

1. My father sold his old car last week.   *sold*

   I bought some paper for my art class.   *bought*

2. My basket is full of shiny red apples.   _____

   The empty shoe boxes are on the steps.   _____

3. We will be riding over a bumpy road.   _____

   The lake looks smooth this morning.   _____

4. Whisper the clue to your partner.   _____

   I heard you shout my name.   _____

Read each pair of sentences. In the blanks, write a pair of synonyms (words that have the same meaning) from the sentences.

1. What kind of present should I make for him?   *present*

   I saved my money to buy her a birthday gift.   *gift*

2. The school is near the city park.   _____

   Does your aunt live close to my friend's home?   _____

3. The teacher read the story to the class.   _____

   Would you like to hear a tale about a rabbit?   _____

4. If we hurry to the school, we can see the show.   _____

   Because we were running out of time, we had to rush.   _____

Review of identification of antonyms and synonyms

Antonyms and Synonyms

Name _____

Read the list of words below. Then read the sentences that follow. Write the word from the list that is an antonym (opposite) for the underlined word in each sentence.

never	float	late
strong	save	bought

1. I would like to <u>spend</u> some money this year. _____ *save* _____

2. Am I here too <u>early</u> to see the show? _____

3. Jake <u>always</u> brings his lunch from home. _____

4. The toy boat will <u>sink</u> when you put it in the water. _____

5. Running races has made my legs feel <u>weak</u>. _____

6. I <u>sold</u> baskets of flowers at the market. _____

Read the list of words below. Then read the sentences that follow. Write the word from the list that is a synonym (word that has the same meaning) for the underlined word in each sentence.

unhappy	cool	glad
present	path	pretty

1. I felt <u>sad</u> when my friend moved. *unhappy*

2. The colored lights of the city look <u>beautiful</u>. _____

3. He made the painting as a <u>gift</u> for his uncle. _____

4. The wind makes me feel <u>chilly</u>. _____

5. I am <u>happy</u> that you could be with us today. _____

6. This <u>trail</u> leads to some picnic tables. _____

Assessment of identifying antonyms and synonyms in context

Homophones

Name _____

| Homophones are words that sound the same but have different spellings and different meanings. | would - wood |

Read the words. Draw a line to match each word with its homophone (word that sounds the same).

your	tow	night	knight	week	hear
toe	you're	knew	tale	here	sent
wait	weight	tail	new	cent	pale
too	sale	deer	dear	pail	weak
sail	two	maid	made	sea	see

Read each pair of sentences. In the blanks, write a pair of homophones (words that sound the same) from the sentences.

1. The book you want is on the right side of the shelf.   *right*

   Please write a letter to me soon.   *write*

2. My nose always gets sunburned when I'm at the beach.   _____

   Edward knows the way to the new classroom.   _____

3. Where can I buy some fishing line for my new rod?   _____

   We went by the street where you used to live.   _____

4. There is a big knot in that jump rope.   _____

   Penny will not be running in the next race.   _____

5. Before I bake bread, I must buy some flour.   _____

   The flower will look nice in this tall yellow vase.   _____

Homographs

Name _____

Homographs are words that have the same spelling but different meanings. Sometimes they are pronounced differently.

Those old pipes are made of **lead.**

Jack will **lead** the band.

Read each pair of sentences and circle the homographs (words that have the same spelling). Then draw a line from each sentence to the picture it tells about.

Connie will show us how to (wind) the clock.

The (wind) made the trees bend near the water.

I could feel the tree's rough bark.

The dog will bark when it sees you.

In the play, he must slowly bow to the queen.

Debbie tied a large bow onto the birthday gift.

Please tear the paper into two pieces.

A tiny tear fell from the baby's eye.

Jack will close the door of the car.

Annie stood close to the basketball hoop.

Homophones and Homographs

Name _____

Read the words below. Circle the two words in each row that are homophones (words that sound the same).

1.	been	(bear)	bake	(bare)	bale
2.	beat	beak	bead	beet	bean
3.	sink	cent	seem	center	scent
4.	I	I've	eye	egg	elf
5.	send	sea	see	sell	seat
6.	heat	head	he	heal	heel

Read the homographs (words that have the same spelling) and their meanings below. Then read the sentences that follow. In each sentence, decide the meaning of the underlined homograph. Write the letter of the correct meaning in the blank.

lead
A. a heavy metal
B. to show the way

tear
A. to rip
B. a drop of water from the eye

close
A. to shut
B. near

1. The pipes in the old building are made of <u>lead</u>. *a*

2. Did I see a <u>tear</u> fall from your eye? _____

3. Russell stood <u>close</u> to his sister. _____

4. Who will <u>lead</u> us to the lake? _____

5. Please <u>close</u> the book when you are done reading the chapter. _____

6. Use the edge of the box to <u>tear</u> the wrapping paper. _____

Identifying homophones; Determining meanings of homographs

Homophones and Homographs

<u>Name</u>

Read each pair of sentences. In the blanks, write a pair of homophones (words that sound the same) from the sentences.

1. I knew you would like to go walking through the city.   *knew*

   The tall building you see on this street is new.   *new*

2. Please meet me at the school lunchroom.   _____

   What kind of meat should I use in the soup?   _____

3. Carry the water in a little pail.   _____

   When I was sick, my face looked pale.   _____

4. You may use this oar in the rowboat.   _____

   Come to my house before or after lunch.   _____

5. I will be sailing for eight days.   _____

   The puppy ate all of its food today.   _____

Read the list of homographs (words that have the same spelling) below. Then read each pair of meanings that follows. Write the homograph from the list that matches both meanings.

    wind   bark   close   tear   bow   lead

1. A. to bend the head or body   B. a knot made of ribbon   *bow*

2. A. to shut   B. near   _____

3. A. moving air   B. to turn or tighten   _____

4. A. water from the eye   B. to rip   _____

Homophones and Homographs

Name _____

Read each pair of sentences. In the blanks, write a pair of homophones (words that sound the same) from the sentences.

1. The cut will heal quickly if it is kept clean.   *heal*

   My left shoe needs a new heel.   *heel*

2. She knew the answer to the question.   _____

   I found the new book on the top of the bookshelf.   _____

3. I rode to the woods on a brown pony.   _____

   Which road leads to the shopping center?   _____

4. The bear cubs in the zoo are so playful.   _____

   I walked in the sand in my bare feet.   _____

Read the homographs (words that have the same spelling) and their meanings below. Then read the sentences that follow. In each sentence, decide the meaning of the underlined homograph. Write the letter of the correct meaning in the blank.

wind	**bow**	**tear**
A. moving air	A. to bend the head or body	A. to rip
B. to turn or twist	B. a knot made of ribbon	B. a drop of water from the eye

1. You need to <u>wind</u> the key on that toy to make it work. *B*

2. Please put a yellow <u>bow</u> on that gift. _____

3. How did you <u>tear</u> your shirt? _____

4. The <u>wind</u> blew the leaves across the lawn. _____

Alphabetical Order

Name _____

You can put words in alphabetical order by looking at the first letter of each word. If the first letters of the words are the same, look at the second letters. If the second letters of the words are the same, look at the third letters.

dr**a**nk
dr**i**ve
dr**u**m

Read the lists of words. Number each list of words in alphabetical order.

List 1		List 2		List 3		List 4	
nail	_1_	price	___	clean	___	bring	___
nut	___	paint	___	city	___	blink	___
nine	___	pink	___	crown	___	broke	___
next	___	put	___	call	___	black	___
night	___	plum	___	coin	___	bread	___
noise	___	pond	___	cent	___	brush	___

Read the groups of words. Write each group of words in alphabetical order.

cream   crumb   cry
cross   crack

hide   home   heat
hall   hunt

shelf   shine   shoe
shut   sharp

1. *crack* _____

2. _____

3. _____

4. _____

5. _____

1. _____

2. _____

3. _____

4. _____

5. _____

1. _____

2. _____

3. _____

4. _____

5. _____

Alphabetizing by second and third letters

Guide Words

Name _____

The two words at the top of a dictionary page are called guide words. The first guide word is the same as the first word listed on the page. The second guide word is the same as the last word listed on the page. To find a word in the dictionary, decide if it comes in alphabetical order between the guide words on a page. If it does, you will find the word on that page.

Read each pair of guide words and the words that are listed below them. Circle the four words in each list that could be found on a page that has those guide words.

draw / foil	**melt / pony**	**boat / cone**
dime	past	crown
(drink)	open	bride
(face)	match	cloud
from	prize	call
(dust)	musl	chain
(fire)	nine	cut

get / heavy	**rose / stand**	**two / wrote**
grow	rich	tractor
happy	slide	turtle
house	rush	under
icy	scarf	voice
give	some	world
goat	return	wind

Guide Words

Name _____

Read the six pairs of guide words and their dictionary page numbers. Then read the lists of words that follow. Write the page number on which each list word would be found in the dictionary.

apple / bend—p. 6 **both / bunch**—p. 8 **flight / give**—p. 26
glove / happy—p. 28 **roar / send**—p. 46 **sink / use**—p. 48

1. as _p. 6_

2. smell _____

3. gaze _____

4. bright _____

5. breeze _____

6. goat _____

7. sand _____

8. grown _____

9. band _____

10. speak _____

11. base _____

12. those _____

13. branch _____

14. geese _____

15. rust _____

16. brown _____

17. art _____

18. grape _____

19. rug _____

20. fresh _____

21. bark _____

22. sold _____

23. rule _____

24. guess _____

Using guide words

Guide Words

Name _____

Read the lists of words below. Then read the guide words that follow. Write each list word below the correct pair of guide words. Then number each list of words to show how they would be listed in alphabetical order.

bench	cane	lunch	change	must
leave	ashes	my	born	city
buy	make	oak	law	barn
noise	nice	answer	chew	lime

1. above / broke

bench   *4*

_____ _____

_____ _____

_____ _____

_____ _____

2. butter / corn

_____ _____

_____ _____

_____ _____

_____ _____

3. lamb / mice

_____ _____

_____ _____

_____ _____

_____ _____

4. mountain / old

_____ _____

_____ _____

_____ _____

_____ _____

Guide Words

Name _____

Read each pair of guide words and the words that are listed below them. Circle the four words in each list that could be found on a page that has those guide words.

held / ink	**jeep / leave**	**mist / nine**	**seat / such**
hall	large	monkey	shelf
hide	jail	march	south
ice	join	name	spare
horse	judge	melt	science
howl	June	myself	swing
itself	lift	neat	smoke

(circled: hide, ice, horse, howl)

Read the four pairs of guide words and their dictionary page numbers. Then read the lists of words that follow. Write the page number on which each list word would be found in the dictionary.

above / are—p. 1   **arm / blue**—p. 2
both / child—p. 5   **cord / dime**—p. 7

1. ate   _p. 2_   8. always _____   15. dawn _____
2. add   _____   9. bush _____   16. bunk _____
3. cost _____   10. air _____   17. aunt _____
4. brick _____   11. desk _____   18. chest _____
5. awake _____   12. angry _____   19. curl _____
6. being _____   13. apple _____   20. cent _____
7. animal _____   14. base _____   21. creek _____

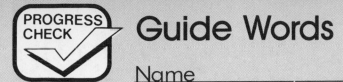
Name _____

Read the lists of words below. Then read the guide words that follow. Write each list word below the correct pair of guide words. Then number each list of words to show how they would be listed in alphabetical order.

knee	heat	valley	idea	twelve
high	upon	listen	its	ice
uncle	jam	lace	jelly	job
lead	lump	hope	join	us

1. **harm / inch**

high   2

_____   ___

_____   ___

_____   ___

_____   ___

2. **is / kept**

_____   ___

_____   ___

_____   ___

_____   ___

_____   ___

3. **kind / mercy**

_____   ___

_____   ___

_____   ___

_____   ___

_____   ___

4. **turn / village**

_____   ___

_____   ___

_____   ___

_____   ___

_____   ___

Assessment of using guide words; Alphabetizing by first, second, and third letters

Name _____

Weather

Everyone talks about the weather, but no one does anything about it. Have you ever heard this saying? There's not much anyone *can* do about the weather. Would you like to have a picnic or go swimming? Do you want to go ice skating or ride your sled? The weather may decide what you can do.

Hot and Cold

In many places, it is hot in the summer. In the winter, it is cold. In the spring and fall, it may be warm on some days and cool on others. Knowing if it will be hot, warm, cool, or cold can help you decide how to dress and what kind of work or play you can do.

Wind

Air that moves sideways is called wind. A wind that blows from the north is cold, and a wind that blows from the south may be warm. The speed of the wind can change the weather.

Clouds

The clouds in the sky can also change the weather. There are different kinds of clouds. Many people can tell from the kind of clouds in the sky what the weather is going to be like. Some clouds mean rain; other clouds mean fair weather.

1. Check the word that tells the main idea.

   _____ picnics   _____ weather   _____ clouds

2. Check each group of words that tells something that can change the weather.

   _____ the speed of the wind

   _____ the kind of clothes you wear

   _____ the kind of clouds in the sky

Application of reading and comprehension skills in a science context

Name _____

3. Check the two sentences in which *wind* sounds the same.

_____ The wind blew my father's hat across the street.

_____ The wind howled loudly throughout the snowstorm.

_____ Please wind the clock before you go to bed tonight.

4. Check the two sentences in which *fair* has the same meaning.

_____ We had a wonderful time at the state fair this summer.

_____ The weather has been fair for three days in a row.

_____ I like to work in the garden when the weather is fair.

5. Tell how the weather might keep you from going to school.

_____

_____

6. Tell about some plans you made that were changed by the weather. What were the plans? What was the weather like? How did you change your plans because of the weather?

_____

_____

_____

_____

_____

_____

Application of thinking and writing skills in a science context

Sounds and Letters

fa**n** **r**a**ke** **tr**ai**n** **j**ar

auto s**aw** h**ay** **c**ar

cent **ch**air du**ck** **b**e**d**

b**ea**n br**ea**d b**ee** **ei**ght

fe**r**n n**ew**s **g**oat pa**ge**

166

Sounds and Letters

lau**gh**	b**i**b	k**ite**	t**ie**
sh**ie**ld	b**ir**d	**kn**ot	la**mb**
ri**ng**	t**o**p	c**oa**t	b**o**n**e**
co**i**n	m**oo**n	b**oo**k	h**or**n
clo**u**d	d**ou**ghnut	**t**o**u**ch	s**ou**p

Sounds and Letters

wind**ow**

cow

toys

ele**ph**ant

scissors

shoe

thin

three

cu**p**

t**u**b**e**

b**ur**n

wheel

write

fl**y**

pon**y**

Beginning Sounds

Name _____

Read the words and name the pictures. Circle the word that names each picture.

goat		van		came	
note		(man)		tame	
vote		can		(game)	
(coat)		tan		name	

(fan)		face		jaw	
can		case		(saw)	
pan		vase		raw	
van		(lace)		law	

Read the sentences. Complete the unfinished word in each sentence by writing the beginning consonant. The word you form must make sense in the sentence.

1. Please _j_oin us when we go camping next weekend.
2. You can _r_ead the map to see where we are going.
3. We will begin our trip in the _m_orning.
4. It will not take us long to set up the _t_ents when we get to the park.
5. When we get to the lake, we will fly _k_ites.
6. We may be able to go _b_ike riding.
7. When it is dark, we will build a _f_ire.
8. I will teach you how to sing a new _s_ong.
9. Will you say "_y_es" and come with us?

Symbol-sound association of words containing initial consonants. Words containing initial consonants in context   5

Beginning Sounds

Name _____

Words to use: tunnel, map, vegetable, camera, desk, pitcher, log, sixteen, garage, needle, carrot, wolf, ribbon, comb, fan, zoo

Look at the pictures. Write the letter or letters that stand for the beginning sound of each picture name.

_f_ork   _n_ail   _w_ink

_z_ipper   _qu_een   _h_ose

Read each sentence and the word beside it. In each line, change the first letter of the word in dark print to form a new word that will make sense in the sentence. Write the word in the blank.

1. I went to a pet show at the school last _night_.   **might**
2. I have never seen so many cats and _dogs_.   **hogs**
3. One boy had a _talking_ bird.   **walking**
4. A small boy brought a basket that held three _kittens_.   **mittens**
5. Another girl had a tank filled with _fish_.   **wish**
6. I even saw a girl showing a pet _pig_.   **big**
7. The _best_ pets were given prizes.   **west**
8. Picking the winners must have been a hard _job_.   **rob**

6   Sound-symbol association of initial consonants. Words containing initial consonants in context

Ending Sounds

Name _____

Read the words and name the pictures. Circle the word that names each picture.

(bib)		tab		can	
bid		(tag)		cap	
big		tan		(car)	
bit		tap		cat	

bud		mat		(hat)	
(bus)		(map)		had	
bun		mad		ham	
bug		man		has	

Read the sentences. Complete the unfinished word in each sentence by writing the ending consonant. The word you form must make sense in the sentence.

1. Let me tell you what I di_d_ last week.
2. I too_k_ my first airplane ride over the city.
3. My ride was one afternoon after schoo_l_.
4. A friend of my da_d_ flew the small plane.
5. From the air I could see the tall buildings on my stree_t_.
6. Each car and bu_s_ that I saw looked like a little toy.
7. I could see the playground and the roo_f_ of our school.
8. Seeing the city from the air was a lot of fu_n_.

Symbol-sound association of words containing final consonants. Words containing final consonants in context   7

Ending Sounds

Name _____

Words to use: bean, mix, chin, tool, boot, dig, cloud, pail, cup

Name the pictures. Write the letter that stands for the ending sound of each picture name.

boo_k_   sea_l_   lea_f_

dru_m_   si_x_   jee_p_

Read each sentence and the word beside it. In each line, change the last letter of the word in dark print to form a new word that will make sense in the sentence. Write the word in the blank.

1. It is not easy to give my little _dog_ a bath.   **dot**
2. I fill a big round _tub_ with soap and warm water.   **tug**
3. When my dog hears the water running, she hides under my _bed_.   **beg**
4. _Then_ I try to get my dog into the water.   **Them**
5. The dog splashes me and gets me as _wet_ as she is.   **web**
6. Her _fur_ looks clean when I am done.   **fun**
7. Before I know it, my dog is in the _mud_ again!   **mug**

8   Sound-symbol association of final consonants. Words containing final consonants in context

169

Beginning and Ending Sounds
Name

Name the pictures. Write the letters that stand for the consonant sounds of each picture name.

s̲eve̲n̲	g̲a̲s̲	f̲oo̲t̲
m̲oo̲n̲	t̲ige̲r̲	b̲ea̲k̲

Read the sentences and the list of words. Write the word from the list that makes sense in each sentence.

1. The summer day was sunny and ___hot___

2. My ___job___ was to catch as many fish as I could.

3. I bought a ___lot___ of bait at the corner store.

4. I took my bait and fishing ___rod___ to the lake.

5. I ___put___ my fish into a pail of water.

6. The ___sun___ was going down as I walked to my tent.

7. After a long day of fishing, it felt good to sleep on my ___cot___

not
sun
lot
put
job
rod
cot
hot
get

Assessment of sound-symbol association of initial and final consonants; Words containing initial and final consonants in context

9

Short Vowels
Name

Read the words and name the pictures. Circle the word that names each picture.

tan / (ten) / tip / top	top / tab / tip / tap	tug / tin / (tag) / tan
ran / (rug) / run / rag	bed / (bag) / big / bug	clap / clam / (clock) / click
pen / pat / pin / (pan)	(step) / stop / ship / shop	not / nest / (net) / nut
(pig) / pen / pin / peg	fans / fist / (fish) / fast	cap / cub / cab / (cup)

10

Symbol-sound association of short-vowel words

Short Vowels
Name

Words to use: man, jet, fan, pen, hog, fox, nut, log, run, tip, pit, hug, pin

Name the pictures. Write the letter that stands for the vowel sound of each picture name.

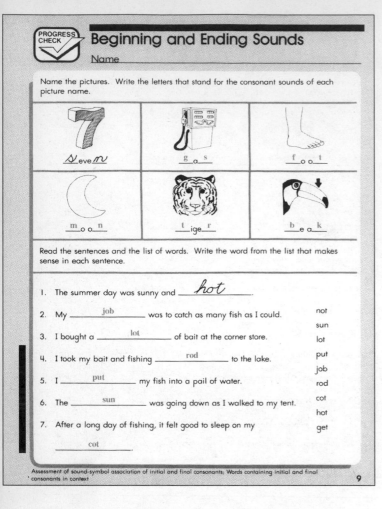

bl_a_ck	l_a_mp	br_u_sh
ch_i_mney	l_o_ck	w_e_ll
d_u_ck	t_e_nt	br_i_ck
h_a_t	p_e_nny	f_o_x

Sound-symbol association of short vowels

11

Short Vowels
Name

Read the words and name the pictures. Circle the word that names each picture.

(tag) / tip / top / tug	(pen) / pit / pot / pan	hot / hat / (hill) / hem
men / (map) / mop / man	luck / lick / (lock) / lack	lad / (leg) / lid / log

Read the sentences. In the blanks below each sentence, write the words from the sentence that have a short-vowel sound. Do not write the words **a** or **the.**

1. These new red pants feel baggy.

   ___red___ ___pants___ ___baggy___

2. My old hat is bright yellow.

   ___hat___ ___is___ ___yellow___

3. My green socks have big stripes.

   ___socks___ ___big___

4. I feel like a funny circus clown.

   ___funny___ ___circus___

12

Symbol-sound association of short-vowel words; Identifying short-vowel words in context

Read each set of sentences and its list of words. Write the word from the list that makes sense in each sentence.

1. Many of my school friends started a _club_.

2. We like to go hiking and _camping_ at nearby places.

3. Tomorrow we _plan_ to go on a hike through the woods.

4. You can meet _us_ early in the morning.

5. You will get hungry, so remember to bring a _lunch_.

6. If you need a backpack, I can _lend_ you one.

7. My father _can_ take us to the park.

club
us
luck
camping
can
plan
stamp
lend
lunch

8. Jack's mom will _bring_ us home.

9. I hope we have a _sunny_ day.

10. We'll talk about the hike the _next_ time we meet.

11. Carlos _will_ show us his pictures.

12. Sally might bring the _rocks_ and leaves she finds.

13. Kim will _tell_ us about other parks.

14. We may want to talk about taking a camping _trip_.

15. When the morning is over, we can eat a _snack_.

jump
will
next
bring
rocks
snack
pick
sunny
tell
trip

Read the sentences. Complete the unfinished word in each sentence by writing the missing vowel. The word you form must make sense in the sentence.

1. I visited the farm animals l_a_st week.

2. I w_e_nt inside the big red barn with my friend Maria.

3. There I saw a large p_i_g sleeping in the corner of a pen.

4. Many young pigs ran around in another large p_e_n.

5. I could tell they liked running in the m_u_d.

6. It was fun to sp_e_nd time looking at the pigs.

7. Outside I saw a b_i_g horse.

8. My friend showed me how it could tr_o_t around the barn.

9. She also showed me how to br_u_sh the horse's coat.

10. The horse l_e_t me pet its nose.

11. Its nose felt warm and s_o_ft.

12. Now I w_i_sh I had a horse of my own.

13. I can't have one in my c_i_ty apartment.

14. So, I'll go b_a_ck to visit the farm again.

Read the words and look at the pictures. Circle the word that tells about each picture.

(bike) bake bite base		cage code cone cane		mile mole (mule) male	
rope rake (robe) ride		like lane lake (line)		(nose) nine note nice	
cove (cane) cave cone		rage robe rode (rake)		cage (cube) cape cute	
dime (dive) date dune		time (tube) tide tune		hope (hive) home hike	

Read the words and look at the pictures. Circle the word that tells about each picture.

rise rope (rose) ripe		(skate) slide snake slope		(home) hide hive hose	
time (tape) take tide		fine fake (five) face		time tile tube (tune)	

Read the sentences. In the blanks below each sentence, write the words from the sentence that have a long-vowel sound. Do not write the words **a** or **the**.

1. I like visiting different places.

   _I_   _like_   _places_

2. Last June I visited another state with a friend.

   June   _I_   _state_

3. We went swimming and rode bikes in a park.

   _We_   _rode_   _bikes_

4. I wrote a tune about our summer trip.

   _I_   _wrote_   _tune_

Long Vowels

Name _____ Words to use: cake, rice, lake, rose, cave, dime, tube, stone, ice, cage, vine, line, note, cane, robe, mule, cone, nine, tube

Look at the pictures. Write the letter or letters that stand for the vowel sound in each picture name.

r__a__ke	r__o__pe	g__a__me
c__u__be	b__i__ke	st__o__ve
n__i__ne	l__a__ce	fl__u__te
r__a__ce	h__i__ve	b__o__ne

Sound-symbol association of long-vowel words   17

Long Vowels

Name _____

Read the sentences. Complete the unfinished word in each sentence by writing the missing vowel. The word you form must make sense in the sentence.

1. It was l__a__te one night when I heard the noise.

2. I had been sleeping, and the noise w__o__ke me.

3. I didn't have a clock, so I'm not sure what t__i__me it was.

4. The wh__i__te light of the moon lit my bedroom.

5. I h__a__te to say that I was feeling afraid.

6. Again I heard the s__a__me sound.

7. I must have looked p__a__le as I sat up in bed.

8. I felt myself starting to sh__a__ke.

9. I remember telling myself to be br__a__ve.

10. I got out of bed and put on a warm r__o__be.

11. I called my cat's n__a__me.

12. A sound c__a__me from the toy box in a corner of my room.

13. Guess who had found a new place to h__i__de?

14. I felt myself begin to sm__i__le.

15. The cat looked c__u__te as she jumped out of the toy box when I opened it.

18   Long-vowel words in context

OLD and IND

Name _____

The letter **o** followed by **ld** usually stands for the long-**o** sound. The letter **i** followed by **nd** usually stands for the long-**i** sound.

c**old**
k**ind**

Read each sentence and words beside it. Write the word that makes sense in each sentence.

1. Did you get _____cold_____ while you were waiting for the bus?
   - cone
   - cold
   - cot

2. When I got a new bike, I _____sold_____ my old one.
   - sold
   - soak
   - sock

3. Would you _____mind_____ going shopping with me?
   - mix
   - mine
   - mind

4. Little children like to _____hold_____ our puppy.
   - hold
   - home
   - hoe

5. Please keep your reading papers in this _____folder_____.
   - colder
   - folder
   - older

6. Were you able to _____find_____ the button you lost?
   - find
   - fin
   - fine

7. What _____kind_____ of eggs shall I cook today?
   - kind
   - king
   - kite

8. Linc said to my teacher, "I am feeling _____fine_____."
   - find
   - fin
   - fine

9. Were you at home when Luis _____told_____ you the news?
   - fold
   - told
   - cold

Words containing old and ind in context   19

OLD and IND

Name _____

Read the sentences and the list of words. Write the word from the list that makes sense in each sentence.

1. It was _____kind_____ of you to walk my dog.

2. The shop on the corner _____sold_____ balloons and kites.

3. The workers will _____grind_____ the meat while you wait.

4. I'm having trouble _____finding_____ my math paper.

5. Do you know where we can buy a candle _____holder_____ to set on our new table?

6. Visiting Denny was the _____kindest_____ thing you could do for him.

7. After we do the wash, we must _____fold_____ the clothes.

8. His ride through the snowstorm showed that the prince was _____bold_____.

9. Would you _____mind_____ if I bring my brother and sister with me?

10. The park worker _____told_____ us about the animals that live in the woods.

11. Seeing-eye dogs are used to lead _____blind_____ persons.

12. I keep all of my school papers in a large _____folder_____.

13. Which of the five bicycles is the _____oldest_____?

- fold
- finding
- told
- blind
- grind
- holder
- oldest
- kind
- bold
- sold
- mind
- kindest
- folder

20   Words containing old and ind in context

Long Vowels

Name _____

Read each set of sentences and its list of words. Write the word from the list that makes sense in each sentence.

1. Last spring I _*wrote*_ a letter to my aunt.
2. I wanted to visit her ___home___ for a week.
3. She said it would be ___nice___ for me to visit.
4. One night I flew there in a huge ___plane___.
5. We were lucky that we didn't have one ___cold___ day.
6. We spent a lot of time ___outside___.
7. I wanted to ___find___ some rocks to take to school.
8. I found many ___pine___ cones, too.

Words
wrote
cold
nice
flute
outside
home
find
plane
told
pine

1. One day I helped my aunt by using a ___rake___ in the garden.
2. For fun, I jumped into a ___pile___ of straw.
3. Each evening, I fed the ___cute___ calf.
4. Before the sun went down, I would ___ride___ the pony.
5. After dinner, my uncle would play a ___tune___ for us on his flute.
6. He showed me how he reads the ___notes___ of each song.

Words
pile
cute
grind
rake
notes
sold
tune
ride

Assessment of long-vowel words in context   21

Short and Long Vowels

Words to use: tape, mice, fish, clock, cold, bike, tug, bib, cent, hole

Name _____

Name the pictures. Write the letter or letters that stand for the vowel sound of each picture name.

f_i_ve	l_a_ke	s_u_n
b_e_d	r_o_pe	f_a_n
r_a_ke	g_o_ld	d_i_me
fl_u_te	p_i_g	t_o_p

22   Sound-symbol association of short- and long-vowel words

Short and Long Vowels

Name _____

Read the sentences. Complete the unfinished word in each sentence by writing the missing vowel or vowels. The word you form must make sense in the sentence.

1. The family garden is in b_a_ck of the house.
2. Every spring, I h_e_lp my mother plant the seeds.
3. First we use a shovel to d_i_g up the soil.
4. We use a r_a_ke to make the soil smooth.
5. Then the seeds are planted in n_i_ne straight rows.
6. The summer s_u_n helps the plants grow.
7. I pick every ripe green bean that I can f_i_nd.
8. We begin going to the market in J_u_ne.
9. We t_a_ke a lot of the food that grew in our garden.
10. The food is s_o_ld from the back of our new truck.
11. I put each person's food in a paper b_a_g.
12. Sometimes I s_i_t and watch the people.
13. The bright shining sun makes me h_o_t.
14. It makes me want to j_u_mp into a lake.
15. That's just what my d_a_d lets me do after we leave the market.

Short- and long-vowel words in context   23

Short and Long Vowels

Name _____

Read each sentence and the words beside it. Write the word that makes sense in each sentence.

1. We should _*stop*_ at Abby's costume shop.
   - stop
   - step
   - stone
2. She will ___let___ us try on some clothes.
   - let
   - led
   - leg
3. You might enjoy looking at the ___masks___.
   - must
   - masks
   - most
4. You'll also like trying on each hat you ___find___.
   - fin
   - find
   - fine
5. I ___like___ to dress up as a big white bunny.
   - like
   - lake
   - line
6. Dressing like a football player is ___fun___, too.
   - fun
   - fan
   - fin
7. My brother looks ___cute___ in an elf costume.
   - cut
   - cute
   - cube
8. If you want to fool people, wear a curly ___wig___.
   - wag
   - wig
   - wide
9. Wouldn't you look strange in long ___pink___ hair?
   - pink
   - pine
   - pin
10. If you want to look like a clown, wear a shiny red ___nose___.
    - nice
    - nose
    - name

24   Short- and long-vowel words in context

Short and Long Vowels

Name _____

Read each set of sentences and its list of words. Write the word from the list that makes sense in each sentence.

1. When we _____camp_____, I like to hike in the nearby woods.

2. I pick up each pine _____cone_____ I see.

3. I sometimes find a bird's _____nest_____ that is filled with eggs.

4. A small animal sometimes comes out of a _____hole_____ in the ground.

5. I carefully watch where I _____step_____.

6. I want the animals to be _____safe_____.

7. Someday I will _____write_____ a story about the things I have seen in the woods.

write
camp
step
ship
cone
mind
safe
nest
hole

1. My grandfather's house is near the bank of a _____pond_____.

2. I feed the _____ducks_____ when I visit.

3. I like to watch them _____swim_____ around.

4. To get sun, they sit on a flat _____rock_____.

5. All the ducks march in a _____line_____.

6. They look so _____cute_____.

7. I _____wish_____ I lived near a pond as Grandfather does.

wish
line
hold
pond
cute
ducks
swim
rock
stamp

Short- and long-vowel words in context   25

PROGRESS CHECK

Short and Long Vowels

Name _____

Read each sentence and the words beside it. Write the word that makes sense in each sentence.

1. Randy will be _____ten_____ years old on his birthday.

ten
tan
ton

2. We are beginning to _____plan_____ a surprise party.

plan
plane
plant

3. Kristy will _____tell_____ our friends about the party.

tall
talk
tell

4. Bobby and Sandy can _____bake_____ a cake.

back
bake
base

5. Jeff will teach us a new _____kind_____ of game.

king
kind
kick

6. Let's make a _____huge_____ sign that says, "Happy Birthday."

hug
huge
hum

7. When it's time, Randy's grandmother will _____send_____ him to the store.

sand
send
sent

8. We will _____hide_____ behind the chairs in his house.

hid
hide
hive

9. Jill will begin the birthday _____tune_____.

tune
tube
tub

10. I _____hope_____ Randy will be surprised!

hope
hop
home

26   Assessment of short- and long-vowel words in context

Hard and Soft C and G

Name _____

The letters **c** or **g** followed by **e, i,** or **y** usually stand for their soft sounds, as in **cent** and **page**. The letters **c** or **g** followed by any other letters usually stand for their hard sounds, as in **cat** and **wagon**.

cent
(soft **c**)

pa**ge**
(soft **g**)

Read the words and name the pictures. Draw a line from each word to the picture it names.

city
cube

game
stage

giraffe
garden

card
celery

pig
cage

calf
face

Symbol-sound association of hard- and soft-c and hard- and soft-g words   27

Hard and Soft C and G

Name _____

Read the lists of words. Notice the sound that **c** or **g** stands for in each word. Then write each word under the correct heading.

cent
(soft **c**)

pa**ge**
(soft **g**)

contest	goose	place	dragon	goat
price	cow	stage	cabin	calf
fence	guess	cab	gentle	judge
bridge	center	wig	edge	excited

Words may be listed in any order.

Hard **c** as in **cat**	Soft **c** as in **cent**
contest	price
cow	fence
cab	center
cabin	place
calf	excited

Hard **g** as in **wagon**	Soft **g** as in **page**
goose	bridge
guess	stage
wig	gentle
dragon	edge
goat	judge

28   Symbol-sound association of hard- and soft-c and hard- and soft-g words

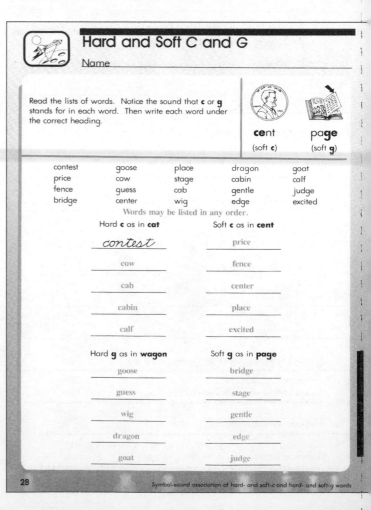

174

Hard and Soft C and G

Name _____

Read the sentences. In the blanks below each sentence, write the words from the sentence that have soft **c** or **g**.

cent	pa**ge**
(soft **c**)	(soft **g**)

1. Gail moved to a city with a well-known bridge.

   city   *bridge*

2. The picture on that page shows a gentle giant.

   page   gentle   giant

3. The judge will hear the first case in this place.

   judge   place

Read the sentences. In the blanks below each sentence, write the words from the sentence that have hard **c** or **g**.

1. Can you get the cat before it runs under the fence?

   Can   *get*   *cat*

2. We raced to catch the goat in the garden.

   catch   goat   garden

3. The cow was excited when it got outside the gate.

   cow   got   gate

Identifying hard- and soft-c and hard- and soft-g words in context   29

Hard and Soft C and G

Name _____

Read the sentences and the words beside them. Write the word that makes sense in each sentence.

1. Please sign this birthday _____*card*_____.
2. We can send it to our friend in the __*city*__.

   city / cost / card

3. Read the words on the first __*page*__ of this book.
4. They tell you how to play a running __*game*__.

   cage / page / game

5. Would you like a __*slice*__ of wheat bread?
6. Should I fill your __*cup*__ with milk?

   cup / cent / slice

7. The park is near the __*bridge*__ that crosses the stream.
8. Wing likes to look at the flower __*garden*__ there.

   bridge / car / garden

9. When the play begins, I am standing on the __*stage*__.
10. She will sing a very __*gentle*__ song.

    wagon / gentle / stage

11. Did you like the animal shows in the __*circus*__?
12. I thought the monkeys were __*cute*__.

    price / circus / cute

13. Do you like the taste of __*rice*__?
14. I can __*cook*__ some for you to try.

    center / cook / rice

30   Review of hard- and soft-c and hard- and soft-g words in context

---

Hard and Soft C and G

Name _____

Read each sentence. Circle the word **hard** or **soft** to tell the kind of sound the **c** or **g** in dark print stands for. Remember: **Cent** and **page** have soft sounds. **Cat** and **wagon** have hard sounds.

1. Where will the cooking **c**ontest be held? (hard) / soft
2. There is a bicycle shop in the **c**enter of the town. hard / (soft)
3. My make-believe story is about an unhappy fro**g**. (hard) / soft
4. What kind of **g**ame should we play? (hard) / soft
5. After he ran two miles his fa**c**e was red. hard / (soft)
6. Will you help me choose a **c**andle? (hard) / soft
7. Her father bought her a new silver bra**c**elet. hard / (soft)
8. Lin wore a long black wi**g** at the costume party. (hard) / soft
9. Do you know the pri**c**e of that football shirt? hard / (soft)
10. The **g**iraffe has a long neck. hard / (soft)
11. Stand away from the ed**g**e of the cliff. hard / (soft)

Assessment of hard- and soft-c and hard and soft-g words   31

Two-Letter Blends

Name _____

Words to use: twist, swim, snack, speed, sting, smell, clap, flip, plug, glide, blink, sleep, brake, toast, blink, drip, grin, cream, print, square

In some words, one consonant follows another consonant. To say these words, blend the sounds of the two consonants together.

stop	**tw**in
play	**squ**irrel
green	

Read the words and look at the pictures. Circle the word that tells about each picture.

(crib) / trip / grin / drip	clock / float / (block) / glove	trap / (snap) / slap / clap
grown / brown / frown / (crown)	stone / (smoke) / spoke / slope	dry / (cry) / fry / pry
flow / glow / slow / (snow)	black / clam / (flag) / glass	spot / slide / stir / (squirrel)
twice / twin / (twine) / twig	flame / plane / slate / (plate)	draw / (tray) / gray / crab

32   Symbol-sound association of words containing tw, s, l, and r blends

175

Two-Letter Blends

Words to use: broom, frost, twin, snap, plum, blink, gray, train

Read each sentence and the words beside it. Write the word that makes sense in each sentence.

1. I like to roller _skate_ outdoors.

state
skate
slate

2. I _start_ at my house and skate to the park.

smart
start
scarf

3. If I think I'm going to fall, I hold onto a _tree_.

free
tree
glee

4. I am careful not to trip on each _crack_ of the sidewalk.

crack
track
black

5. The smooth path in the park helps me to _glide_.

glide
twin
slid

6. My arms _swing_ as I skate along the path.

sting
swing
skip

7. The soft _breeze_ feels good in my hair.

breeze
freeze
green

8. I sometimes _dream_ about flying through the air.

great
twenty
dream

9. I meet two people on the path and _squeeze_ between them.

sweater
squeeze
speech

10. After skating I am tired, but I feel _great_!

great
cream
treat

Words containing tw, s, l, and r blends in context

33

Two-Letter Blends

Name

Words to use: twenty, swell, spoke, spark, stamp, smile, cloud, flower, plate, squeeze, drink, prize, gray

Read the sentences. Complete the unfinished word in each sentence by writing the missing blend. Choose from the following blends: **sw, cl, fl, br, fr, sq.** The word you form must make sense in the sentence.

1. Please help me _cl_ean my dirty bedroom.

2. I will pick up the clothes from the _fl_oor.

3. Would you _sw_eep the floor with this broom?

4. My brother's toy _sq_uirrel is under the bed.

5. Here is the _br_ush that I thought was lost.

6. Now I can walk _fr_om place to place without tripping over things!

Read the sentences. Complete the unfinished word in each sentence by writing the missing blend. Choose from the following blends: **tw, sc, sn, sp, st, gl, sl.** The word you form must make sense in the sentence.

1. Grandfather will _sc_old me if I get up.

2. He said I should try to _sl_eep.

3. I guess he heard me _sn_eezing this morning.

4. My _tw_in sister had a cold before I did.

5. She had to _sp_end two days in bed last weekend.

6. She told me that Grandfather can also tell a good _st_ory any time of day.

7. I am _gl_ad that Grandfather is here.

34

Words containing tw, s, l, and r blends in context

Two-Letter Blends

REVIEW

Name

Read each clue. Complete the word beside it to form a word that matches the clue. Choose from the following blends: **tw, sl, sm, st, sw.** You may use a blend more than once.

1. something you need to mail a letter _st_amp

2. the number before thirteen _tw_elve

3. a toy used to ride on snow _sl_ed

4. something you can do in a pool or lake _sw_im

5. to mix food _st_ir

6. something you do when you are happy _sm_ile

Read each clue. Complete the word beside it to form a word that matches the clue. Choose from the following blends: **bl, fl, br, gr, tr, cr, sq.**

1. the color of the sky _bl_ue

2. a path _tr_ail

3. a kind of fruit that grows on a vine _gr_ape

4. something that hangs on a pole _fl_ag

5. something that can be made into toast _br_ead

6. a shape that has four sides of the same length _sq_uare

7. a loud noise _cr_ash

Review of words containing tw, s, l, and r blends

35

Three-Letter Blends

Name

In some words, the letter **s** is followed by two other consonants. To say these words, blend the sound of **s** with the sounds of the consonants that follow.

spring
scream
split
strip

Read the words and look at the pictures. Circle the word that tells about each picture.

split
(string)
spring
strip

strange
sprang
(splash)
scratch

stream
spread
(screw)
street

split
(splinter)
strip
strike

street
scream
stream
(spread)

(spray)
scratch
strange
sprang

screech
spread
stream
(street)

splash
(scratch)
straight
sprang

spread
scream
(stream)
street

sprout
(strong)
scrap
stroke

spray
scrape
(straw)
splash

strange
(scrape)
splash
sprang

36

Symbol-sound association of words containing three-letter blends: spr, scr, spl, str

---

176

Three-Letter Blends

Name _____

Words to use: spray, spread, sprout, sprain, scrap, screen, split, stripe, straight, screech, scratch, splash, strong, splinter, strip

Read each sentence and the words beside it. Write the word that makes sense in each sentence.

1. What a _**strange**_ day I've had today!

    scratch / strange / sprang

2. I _**split**_ a seam in my yellow shirt.

    strike / split / strip

3. I _**spread**_ butter on my hand instead of on the toast.

    stream / spread / scream

4. My best friend _**sprained**_ his leg when we were playing.

    stranger / sprained / screamed

5. I forgot to get a _**straw**_ for my milk when I went through the lunch line.

    strange / straw / straight

6. The _**strap**_ on my only backpack broke.

    splash / strap / scratch

7. I ran into the _**screen**_ door.

    stream / screen / spread

8. I got a _**splinter**_ in my right hand.

    splinter / strip / strike

9. A car _**splashed**_ water on me.

    scraped / splashed / scratched

10. I think I'll go _**straight**_ to bed when I get home!

    spray / scratch / straight

Words containing three-letter blends in context: spr, scr, spl, str   37

Three-Letter Blends

Name _____

Read the sentences. Complete the unfinished word in each sentence by writing the missing blend. Choose from the following blends: **spr, scr, spl, str.** You may use a blend more than once. The word you form must make sense in the sentence.

1. Would you like to fix _**scr**_ambled eggs for Grandmother?

2. Can Brenda swim _**str**_aight across the deep end of the pool?

3. Try not to make a big _**spl**_ash when you dive.

4. I used the hose to _**spr**_ay water for the children.

5. Last spring I helped put a new _**scr**_een in my window.

6. How did Jan _**spr**_ain her arm?

7. We plan to plant some flowers next _**spr**_ing.

8. Before winter, we _**spl**_it wood to burn in our fireplace.

9. Before we begin painting the house, we must _**scr**_ape off the old paint.

10. Scott let out a loud _**scr**_eam when you frightened him.

11. Listen to that _**str**_ange noise.

12. Is Allan _**str**_ong enough to lift this box?

13. The first time Billy was up to bat, he got a _**str**_ike.

14. How did you get that _**spl**_inter in your finger?

15. Are there any fish in that shallow _**str**_eam?

38   Words containing three-letter blends in context: spr, scr, spl, str

---

Three-Letter Blends

REVIEW

Name _____

Read each clue. Complete the word beside it to form a word that matches the clue. Choose from the following blends: **spr, scr, spl, str.** You may use a blend more than once.

1. to hurt an arm or leg by twisting it   _**spr**_ain

2. not curved   _str_aight

3. something cats do with their claws   _scr_atch

4. a wide brook   _str_eam

5. to hurt the skin on a knee   _scr_ape

6. to wash with a brush   _scr_ub

7. what water does when you jump into a pool   _spl_ashes

8. something found in a barn   _str_aw

9. a time of year when flowers bloom outdoors   _spr_ing

10. a tiny piece of wood   _spl_inter

11. another name for a road   _str_eet

12. to yell in a high voice   _scr_eam

13. to put butter on bread   _spr_ead

14. to break something apart   _spl_it

15. to scatter tiny drops of water   _spr_ay

Review of words containing three-letter blends: spr, scr, spl, str   39

Ending Blends

Name _____

Words to use: grand, task, sort, sift, ask, desk, spend, mask, rent, bump, skirt, left, lift

At the end of some words two consonants appear together. To say these words, blend the sounds of the two consonants together.

la**st**	sta**mp**
ha**nd**	gi**ft**

Read the words and name the pictures. Circle the word that names each picture.

gasp / **(gift)** / golf / gust	cast / camp / cent / cost	soft / sand / **(sink)** / sent
mast / mist / **(mask)** / milk	pink / **(plant)** / pump / pant	bump / **(belt)** / built / best
rent / **(raft)** / ramp / rest	bank / bent / bend / **(band)**	**(lamp)** / left / lump / lift
stamp / stand / **(stump)** / stunt	**(shelf)** / shirt / shift / skunk	skunk / skirt / shift / **(shirt)**

40   Symbol-sound association of words containing final blends.

Ending Blends

Name _____

Words to use: camp, past, blend, dent, lend, bank, lump, art

Read each sentence and the words beside it. Write the word that makes sense in each sentence.

1. You need to put on old pants and a _shirt_ .
   - shift
   - shirt
   - shelf

2. I want you to go with me to see what's __left__ in the old barn.
   - lift
   - left
   - lamp

3. You can __help__ me open the heavy sliding door.
   - honk
   - help
   - hand

4. I'll see if I can find a __lamp__ to give us some light.
   - land
   - lamp
   - last

5. Look at the rusty tools on this __shelf__ .
   - short
   - shelf
   - shift

6. Do you think Grandfather used this tool to __plant__ seeds?
   - plant
   - part
   - paint

7. She wants to know what kind of bird __built__ that nest.
   - belt
   - built
   - bold

8. We will have to __ask__ our teacher.
   - ask
   - ant
   - and

9. I can __send__ him a letter tonight.
   - send
   - sent
   - self

10. Let's go to the old __fort__ on our next visit.
    - fast
    - fort
    - first

Words containing final blends in context

41

Ending Blends

Name _____

Words to use: hand, paint, mint, list, round, wink, gulf, hurt, link, stand

Complete the unfinished word in each sentence by writing the missing blends. Choose from the following blends: **lf, lt, st, mp, nk, rt, ft, nd, nt, sk.** You may use a blend more than once. The word you form must make sense in the sentence.

1. My friends met our family at the city airpo__rt__ .

2. A strong wi__nd__ was blowing.

3. We ran to put the bags into the tru__nk__ of the car.

4. We stayed at my friend's home because we fe__lt__ it was too cold to camp.

5. First I put a funny ma__sk__ on my face.

6. Next I'll put on a wig made of so__ft__ yellow yarn.

7. I will wear a bright red shi__rt__ and baggy blue pants.

8. Then I'll be ready to go to work in the circus te__nt__ .

9. Most of the books that tell how the old fo__rt__ was built have been sold.

10. There aren't many left on the she__lf__ .

11. People must like the pictures drawn by the book's arti__st__ .

12. They sit at the de__sk__ in the bookstore and look at the books.

13. Please put a sta__mp__ on this letter.

14. I will se__nd__ it to Mom after we go swimming.

15. She will want to know about the ra__ft__ ride we took on the river.

42

Words containing final blends in context

REVIEW

Ending Blends

Name _____

Read each clue. Complete the word beside it to form a word that matches the clue. Choose from the following blends: **st, sk, nd, nk, nt, mp, lf, lt, rt, ft.** You may use a blend more than once.

1. a small lake — po__nd__

2. to spread color with a brush — pai__nt__

3. a tiny, make-believe person — e__lf__

4. what is left of a tree after it has been cut down — stu__mp__

5. a place to save money — ba__nk__

6. the part of the body that pumps blood — hea__rt__

7. the plaster covering on a broken arm or leg — ca__st__

8. a present — gi__ft__

9. the opposite of right — le__ft__

10. something found at a beach — sa__nd__

11. a place for airplanes — airpo__rt__

12. a penny — ce__nt__

13. a group of people who play songs while marching — ba__nd__

14. a table used for writing or studying — de__sk__

15. a young male horse — co__lt__

Review of words containing final blends

43

PROGRESS CHECK ✓

Blends

Name _____

Read each set of sentences and its list of words. Write the word from the list that makes sense in each sentence.

1. Patty walks to the _pond_ in the park.
2. Her dog runs __past__ her.
3. The dog likes to __splash__ water on itself.
4. Patty calls, and the dog runs __straight__ to her.
5. Patty __squeals__ as her dog jumps up.
6. She throws a __stick__ into the air.
7. That dog likes to __play__ "catch."

- play
- straight
- squeals
- stick
- pond
- splash
- draw
- past
- plan

1. One day last week I was standing in __front__ of the house.
2. I saw something __start__ to move.
3. What was that __strange__ animal?
4. I moved slowly and tried to get __close__ to it.
5. I was surprised to see a __skunk__ !
6. I've always been afraid of their __smell__ .
7. "Oh, __please__ don't let it spray me," I thought.
8. I was lucky that I didn't __scream__ .

- close
- skunk
- smell
- free
- front
- scream
- block
- strange
- start
- please

44

Assessment of words containing initial and final blends in context

178

Silent Consonants: KN, WR, and SC

In some words, two consonants together stand for one sound.
The letters **kn** usually stand for the sound of **n**, as in **knot**.
The letters **wr** usually stand for the sound of **r**, as in **write**.
The letters **sc** sometimes stand for the sound of **s**, as in **scissors**.

knot
write
scissors

Look at the pictures. Write the letters that stand for the beginning sound of each picture name.

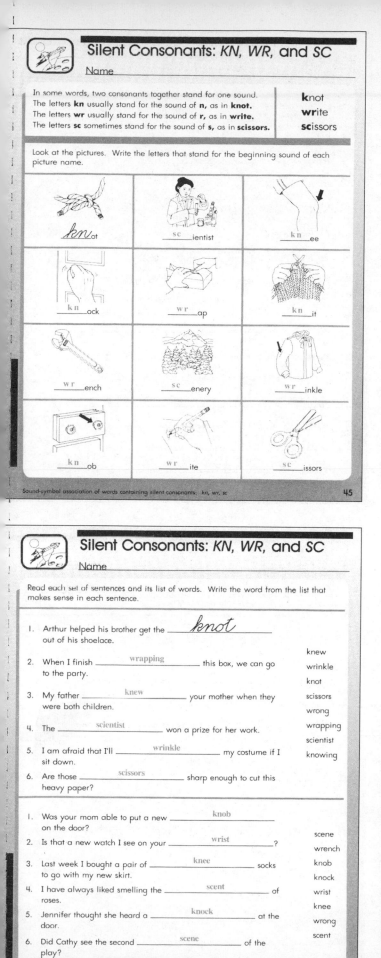

_kn_ot	___sc_ientist	_kn_ee
_k n_ock	_wr_ap	_kn_it
_wr_ench	_sc_enery	_wr_inkle
_k n_ob	_wr_ite	_sc_issors

Sound-symbol association of words containing silent consonants: kn, wr, sc — 45

Silent Consonants: KN, WR, and SC

Name _____

Read each sentence and the words beside it. Write the word that makes sense in each sentence.

1. I left my _science_ book lying on the kitchen table.
   - science / scene / scent

2. What kind of _knife_ is good for cutting apples?
   - know / knife / knee

3. Who will be acting in the _scene_ that takes place in the garden?
   - scissors / science / scene

4. A _wreath_ made of pine cones hangs on the front door.
   - wrote / wren / wreath

5. The bird in that tree is a _wren_.
   - write / wren / wreath

6. Please bring paper, pens, and _scissors_ to art class.
   - scent / scissors / science

7. You will need to bring yellow yarn to the first _knitting_ class.
   - kneeling / knitting / knocking

8. Can we _wrap_ something as big as a bicycle?
   - wrap / wrong / wren

9. The people in the front row will _kneel_ for the picture.
   - knew / kneel / know

10. Do you _know_ how many people plan to come to the party?
    - know / knit / knock

46 — Words containing silent consonants in context: kn, wr, sc

---

Silent Consonants: KN, WR, and SC

Name _____

Read each set of sentences and its list of words. Write the word from the list that makes sense in each sentence.

1. Arthur helped his brother get the _knot_ out of his shoelace.

2. When I finish _wrapping_ this box, we can go to the party.

3. My father _knew_ your mother when they were both children.

4. The _scientist_ won a prize for her work.

5. I am afraid that I'll _wrinkle_ my costume if I sit down.

6. Are those _scissors_ sharp enough to cut this heavy paper?

knew
wrinkle
knot
scissors
wrong
wrapping
scientist
knowing

1. Was your mom able to put a new _knob_ on the door?

2. Is that a new watch I see on your _wrist_?

3. Last week I bought a pair of _knee_ socks to go with my new skirt.

4. I have always liked smelling the _scent_ of roses.

5. Jennifer thought she heard a _knock_ at the door.

6. Did Cathy see the second _scene_ of the play?

scene
wrench
knob
knock
wrist
knee
wrong
scent

Words containing silent consonants in context: kn, wr, sc — 47

Silent Consonants: CK, MB, and GH

Name _____

In some words, two consonants together stand for one sound.
The letters **ck** usually stand for the sound of **k**, as in **duck**.
The letters **mb** usually stand for the sound of **m**, as in **lamb**. The letters **gh** are usually silent, as in **night**.

du**ck**
la**mb**
ni**gh**t

Read the list of words below. Then look at the pictures. Write a word from the list that tells about each picture.

truck	eight	comb	climb	block
brick	light	clock	thumb	

climb	brick	comb
light	truck	clock
eight	thumb	block

48 — Symbol-sound association of words containing silent consonants: ck, mb, gh

179

Read each sentence and the words beside it. Write the word that makes sense in each sentence.

1. The little *chicks* followed their mother.
   - sticks
   - chicks
   - thick

2. My teacher _____taught_____ Allen how to play the drums.
   - eight
   - taught
   - sight

3. Andrew will _____comb_____ his hair before his picture is taken.
   - comb
   - climb
   - thumb

4. How many times can you run around the _____track_____?
   - pack
   - track
   - back

5. Our family _____might_____ take a trip this summer.
   - might
   - sight
   - right

6. Before the grass is cut, we must walk around the yard and pick up each _____stick_____.
   - thick
   - stick
   - lick

7. Each fire fighter must _____climb_____ the ladder.
   - thumb
   - climb
   - comb

8. We ate dinner on our plane _____flight_____ to the city.
   - bright
   - fright
   - flight

9. The children have fun with these building _____blocks_____.
   - blocks
   - socks
   - locks

10. Did you hurt your _____thumb_____ with the hammer?
    - climb
    - thumb
    - comb

Words containing silent consonants in context: ck, mb, gh   49

Read each set of sentences and its list of words. Write the word from the list that makes sense in each sentence.

1. I was able to hold a *lamb* when I visited the zoo.
2. The new house is made of _____bricks_____.
3. The little child covered with mud was quite a _____sight_____.
4. Do I have a hole in the toe of my _____sock_____?
5. Are you seven or _____eight_____ years old?
6. Jess plans on _____climbing_____ that mountain.
7. Is the sun always so _____bright_____ in this window?
8. The dump _____truck_____ can carry a heavy load.

- bright
- sock
- night
- truck
- lamb
- thumb
- eight
- climbing
- sight
- bricks

1. In the winter, the birds eat the bread _____crumbs_____ we give them.
2. He was surprised when he _____caught_____ the ball.
3. We cannot ride our bicycles until it is _____light_____ outside.
4. The gift was a brush and _____comb_____ set.
5. How _____high_____ is the new downtown building?
6. Did you _____check_____ to see that the lights are off?
7. We heard them _____sigh_____ when the race was over.

- comb
- light
- check
- block
- high
- crumbs
- sigh
- climb
- caught

50   Words containing silent consonants in context: ck, mb, gh

---

Read each clue. Write **kn, wr, sc, ck, mb,** or **gh** to complete the word that matches the clue.

1. a time to sleep — ni_gh_t
2. painted scenes used in a play — _sc_enery
3. the flying of a plane or a jet — fli_gh_t
4. to make something with yarn — _kn_it
5. the part of the arm near the hand — _wr_ist
6. something used to make hair smooth — co_mb_
7. a baby sheep — la_mb_
8. the middle part of the leg — _kn_ee
9. a stone — ro_ck_
10. to put words down on paper — _wr_ite
11. not low — hi_gh_
12. something you do to get into a tree — cli_mb_
13. something a train moves on — tra_ck_
14. a tool used to tighten nuts and bolts — _wr_ench
15. the smell of something — _sc_ent

Review of words containing silent consonants: kn, wr, sc, ck, mb, gh   51

Read the list of words below. Then read the sentences that follow. Write the word from the list that makes sense in each sentence.

crumbs	lock	knob	wrinkle	knock	science	wrap
quick	eight	scene	taught	thumb	straight	knew

1. If you _____knock_____ three times, we'll let you into the clubhouse.
2. She twisted the _____knob_____ to turn on the television.
3. Danny painted a beautiful _____scene_____ of the mountains.
4. If we are _____quick_____, we can catch the morning train.
5. Aunt Joyce knew we had been eating because there were _____crumbs_____ on the table.
6. Be careful not to _____wrinkle_____ your new shirt.
7. The children learned about plants in _____science_____ class.
8. The holes in the scissors are for your finger and your _____thumb_____.
9. Chee _____taught_____ his little sister how to tie her shoes.
10. What should Cindy use to _____wrap_____ the food for our lunches?
11. This bicycle path goes _____straight_____ through the city.
12. So far, we have only _____eight_____ persons playing on our team.
13. Be sure to _____lock_____ the car door before you go shopping.
14. I _____knew_____ you would like reading that book.

52   Assessment of words containing silent consonants: kn, wr, sc, ck, mb, gh

180

Vowel Pairs: *AI*, *AY*, and *EI*

Name _____

In some words, two vowels together stand for one vowel sound. The letters **ai** and **ay** usually stand for the long-**a** sound, as in **train** and **hay**. The letters **ei** sometimes stand for the long-**a** sound, as in **eight**.

tr**ai**n
h**ay**
eight

Read the words and look at the pictures. Circle the word that tells about each picture.

sail / (train) / say / tray	tray / (chain) / train / chair	say / (sail) / stay / sprain
braid / trail / brain / (tray)	drain / (playground) / paint / daisy	(hay) / chain / hair / claim
wail / stay / (weigh) / sail	sail / say / stay / (sleigh)	fail / vein / faint / (veil)
sprain / stay / (spray) / stain	pay / pail / (paint) / play	weight / (eight) / sleigh / weigh

Symbol-sound association of words containing vowel digraphs: ai, ay, ei   53

Vowel Pairs: *AI*, *AY*, and *EI*

Name _____

Read each sentence and words beside it. Write the word that makes sense in each sentence.

1. How long must we wait for the afternoon _*train*_ ?
   tray / tail / train

2. What kind of _freight_ do trains and planes carry?
   reigns / freight / sleigh

3. Can you teach me how to _braid_ my hair?
   braid / chain / grain

4. You can carry the dishes to the table on a _tray_ .
   train / tray / tail

5. The nurse wrote my _weight_ on a chart.
   freight / weight / sleigh

6. Could you help me get the _nail_ out of the board?
   nail / sail / tail

7. The children liked the story about the well-known _reindeer_ that could fly.
   reindeer / freight / weight

8. Some people _spray_ water on their plants.
   say / straight / spray

9. Can you _stay_ at my house when your family goes away?
   stain / stay / sleigh

10. Do you know how to fix a bicycle _chain_ ?
    braid / chain / train

54   Words containing vowel digraphs in context: ai, ay, ei

Vowel Pairs: *AI*, *AY*, and *EI*

Name _____

Read the list of words below. Then read the sentences that follow. Write the word from the list that makes sense in each sentence.

weight	crayons	daisy	playground	aim
stay	trail	sleigh	mail	highway
neighbor	eighteen	way		

1. We count cars when our family drives on the _*highway*_

2. Who will pick up your _mail_ at the post office when you are out of town?

3. You can score a point if you _aim_ the basketball at the rim.

4. Growing flowers is something my _neighbor_ does well.

5. If you walk on this dusty _trail_ , you will come to Oak Lake.

6. Where will you _stay_ when you go on your trip to the city?

7. When it snows, Mrs. Bobbitt takes children on _sleigh_ rides through the woods.

8. You can find scissors, paper, and many _crayons_ in my desk.

9. If you want to play kickball, meet on the school _playground_

10. There are _eighteen_ boys and girls in that club.

11. Yoko put a _daisy_ in her hair.

12. Which _way_ should I turn when I get to the school?

13. As I grow taller, I will gain _weight_

Words containing vowel digraphs in context: ai, ay, ei   55

Vowel Pairs: *EE*, *EA*, *OA*, and *OW*

Name _____

In some words, two vowels together stand for one vowel sound. The letters **ee** usually stand for the long-**e** sound, as in **bee**. The letters **ea** can stand for the long-**e** sound, as in **bean** or the short-**e** sound, as in **bread**. The letters **oa** and **ow** often stand for the long-**o** sound, as in **coat** and **window**.

b**ee**
b**ea**n
br**ea**d
c**oa**t
wind**ow**

Read the words and name the pictures. Circle the word that names each picture.

beak / (bee) / bow / boat	green / (goat) / grow / groan	bowl / bread / boat / (beach)
seek / sneak / (snow) / seat	head / heat / (heel) / heavy	loaf / (leaf) / lean / low
sheep / (shadow) / show / sheet	bee / beak / (bread) / beach	boat / beat / bean / (bowl)
three / (thread) / throat / throw	row / read / roast / (road)	tea / teeth / (tree) / treat

56   Symbol-sound association of words containing vowel digraphs: ee, ea, oa, ow

Vowel Pairs: EE, EA, OA, and OW

Name _____

Read each sentence and the words beside it. Write the word that makes sense in each sentence.

1. Do you know how to tie a ___*bow*___ ?

bow
beak
bee

2. I fixed the ___wheel___ of my bicycle.

wheat
wheel
week

3. Would you like some butter or jelly on your ___toast___ ?

toast
team
teeth

4. You may have some eggs for ___breakfast___ .

bread
breakfast
breath

5. Our basketball ___team___ works hard when it plays.

team
tow
teen

6. Today we'll have ___cheese___ and crackers for our snack.

cheek
cheese
cheap

7. The school nurse says I am very ___healthy___ .

heats
healthy
heel

8. That dish can be cleaned with ___soap___ and water.

soap
seed
seal

9. When my uncle sees me he always says, "My, how you've ___grown___ ."

grown
green
greet

10. We will go swimming at the ___beach___ behind our neighbor's house.

beak
beach
been

Vowel Pairs: EE, EA, OA, and OW

Name _____

Read the list of words below. Then read the sentences that follow. Write the word from the list that makes sense in each sentence.

need	teeth	heavy	show	bowl
reach	steep	float	goat	teacher
grow	meant	feather	roast	

1. Jane will be happy to ___*show*___ you her drawing.

2. We had fun feeding the playful ___goat___ at the zoo.

3. The chart on the classroom wall was made by the ___teacher___ .

4. We were careful when we climbed the ___steep___ hill.

5. The basket of apples was too ___heavy___ for me to carry.

6. Justin ___meant___ to call you this morning.

7. My little sister tried to ___reach___ the books on the highest shelf.

8. When we were in the swimming pool, my dad showed me how to ___float___ .

9. The dentist checks my ___teeth___ twice a year.

10. Will I ___need___ eggs to make the muffins?

11. Let's put the popcorn in this yellow ___bowl___ .

12. This daisy will ___grow___ to be as tall as the fence.

13. I found a bird's ___feather___ on the beach.

14. How long will it take to ___roast___ the meat in this oven?

Vowel Pairs: EE, EA, OA, and OW

Name _____

Read each sentence and look at the vowel pairs beside it. Write one of the vowel pairs to complete the unfinished word in each sentence. The word you form must make sense in the sentence.

1. Put on your heavy c___oa___t before we go outside.   oa, ea

2. I can hear the wind bl___ow___ing.   ee, ow

3. Let's walk on this winding r___oa___d that leads to the barn.   oa, ee

4. We will give the horse a tr___ea___t.   ea, ow

5. The horse likes to eat ___oa___ts from our hands.   ea, oa

6. Don't you think its fun to ___ow___n a horse?   ow, ee

1. It's always pl___ea___sant to think about a summer trip.   oa, ea

2. I like to dr___ea___m about the many places I want to visit.   ea, ow

3. Sometime I'd like to take a long b___oa___t trip so I could see the sights.   ea, oa

4. I have always m___ea___nt to plan a train trip to the West.   ow, ea

5. The train I want to ride would have a place for me to sl___ee___p.   ee, ow

---

Vowel Pairs: OO, AU, AW, and EW

Name _____

In some words, two vowels together stand for one sound. The letters **oo** can stand for the sound you hear in the middle of **moon** or **book**. The letters **au** usually stand for the sound you hear at the beginning of **auto**. The letters **aw** usually stand for the sound you hear at the end of **saw**. The letters **ew** usually stand for the sound you hear in the middle of **news**.

m**oo**n
b**oo**k
auto
s**aw**
n**ew**s

Read the words and look at the pictures. Circle the word that tells about each picture.

(book)		screw		(faucet)	
boot		school		few	
blew		(straw)		fault	
broom		spoon		flew	
droop		claw		(hook)	
(draw)		jaw		haul	
dew		(jewel)		hoop	
dawn		chew		hood	
food		lawn		(pool)	
fool		look		straw	
flew		(launch)		paw	
(foot)		law		spoon	
saw		blew		noon	
(screw)		(boot)		blew	
soon		book		(news)	
straw		brook		book	

182

Read each sentence and the words beside it. Write the word that makes sense in each sentence.

1. The light of the __moon__ was bright last night.		mew moon moose
2. I believe there are a __few__ tickets left for the show.		fawn few fault
3. Patrick __stood__ in the rain and waited for the bus.		spoon scoop stood
4. We will get up at __dawn__ to catch the early morning train.		dawn dew draw
5. What kind of __sauce__ should we make for the meat?		sauce screw straw
6. Colleen __drew__ a picture of the snowy mountains.		dew drew droop
7. Does that __rooster__ crow every morning?		raccoon spoon rooster
8. The new speed __law__ helps keep the highways safe.		look launch law
9. Marty hit a fly ball, and Benny __caught__ it.		caught claw cause
10. Richard __shook__ the coins out of his piggy bank.		shook straw sauce

Words containing vowel digraphs in context: oo, au, aw, ew   61

Read the list of words below. Then read the sentences that follow. Write the word from the list that makes sense in each sentence.

cause	look	yawn	flew	daughter
hawk	few	kangaroo	hook	taught
tooth	drawings	spoon	grew	

1. The baby needs a __spoon__ for the food.

2. His little sister just lost a front __tooth__.

3. I __yawn__ when I get up too early in the morning.

4. Martin likes to make __drawings__ of birds and flowers.

5. Please hang your coat on the __hook__ behind the door.

6. Can you tell me if that bird is a __hawk__?

7. The princess is the __daughter__ of the queen.

8. My aunt will __look__ for a new car today.

9. My teacher __taught__ me how to add numbers.

10. Do you have a __few__ minutes to listen to my tape?

11. When my family visited the zoo, my brother wanted to see a baby __kangaroo__ in its mother's pouch.

12. Do the fire fighters know the __cause__ of the fire?

13. A hot-air balloon __flew__ over the fairgrounds this morning.

14. The farmers __grew__ more corn this year than last.

62   Words containing vowel digraphs in context: oo, au, aw, ew

---

Read each sentence and look at the vowel pairs beside it. Write one of the vowel pairs to complete the unfinished word in each sentence. The word you form must make sense in the sentence.

1. There is much to do after sch__oo__l.   oo, au

2. You may plan to play baseball on the front l__aw__n.   aw, ew

3. The swimming p__oo__l is open.   oo, au

4. You can check out a b__oo__k from the library.   oo, aw

5. You'll need to p__au__se and think about what you'd like to do.   au, oo

1. One day we got up at d__aw__n.   aw, oo

2. A f__ew__ of us quickly got dressed.   aw, ew

3. We had planned a walk in the w__oo__ds.   oo, au

4. Our leader had t__au__ght us about animal tracks.   oo, au

5. Before long, Danny s__aw__ some small tracks.   oo, aw

6. We were following a family of racc__oo__ns.   au, oo

Words containing vowel digraphs in context: oo, au, aw, ew   63

Read the list of words below. Then read the sentences that follow. Write the word from the list that makes sense in each sentence.

bread	train	stay	speak	steep	soon	keep
book	draw	few	jewel	own	road	drew

1. I would like to make some __bread__ for my neighbor.

2. Can you __stay__ here awhile and help me bake a loaf?

3. I need a map that shows the __road__ where the shops are.

4. Please __draw__ the map with a marker on this sheet of paper.

5. Will you __keep__ these tickets for me until I'm ready to go?

6. I will be taking a __train__ ride into the city to see your daughter.

7. Nancy got a __book__ from the library today.

8. Someday she would like to have her __own__ set of books.

9. My aunt and uncle have a __few__ horses and cows.

10. They will also have sheep at their ranch __soon__.

11. Andrew __drew__ a picture of a fancy crown.

12. A beautiful __jewel__ was in the center of the crown.

13. Are you able to __speak__ to the group at this week's meeting?

14. We would like to hear about the __steep__ mountain you climbed.

64   Review of words containing vowel digraphs in context: ai, ay, ee, ea, oa, ow, oo, ow, ew

183

Tie has the long-**i** sound spelled by the letters **ie**. **Shield** has the long-**e** sound spelled by the letters **ie**.

tie   shield

Read the words and look at the pictures. Circle the word that tells about each picture.

(tie) / lie	die / (pie)	lie / (necktie)
tield / (lie)	niece / (movie)	chief / (thief)
(field) / movie	die / (chief)	piece / (die)
(cookie) / tie	(piece) / pie	field / (shield)

Symbol-sound association of words containing *ie*

65

Read the list of words. Notice the sound that **ie** stands for in each word. Then write each word under the correct heading.

tie   shield

| field | lie | niece | thief |
| necktie | pie | die | movie |

Order of words may vary.

Long **i** as in **tie**	Long **e** as in **shield**
necktie	field
lie	niece
pie	thief
die	movie

Read the sentences. Complete each sentence by writing a word from the exercise above. The word you write must make sense in the sentence.

1. His __*necktie*__ matched the color of his jacket.

2. We like to pick wild flowers from the __field__ near our home.

3. Would you like to __lie__ down and rest?

4. Her family watched an exciting __movie__ about runners.

5. What made that plant __die__?

6. My __niece__ has a beautiful smile.

7. The __thief__ had taken the important papers.

56   Symbol-sound association of words containing *ie*; Words containing *ie* in context

---

Read the sentences and the list of words. Write the word from the list that makes sense in each sentence.

tie   shield

1. Mindy will __tie__ string around the ball.

2. I would like to be the __chief__ of the fire fighters.

3. I __believe__ you can run the race faster than you ever have before.

4. Should my dad wear a __necktie__ tonight?

5. The grass will __die__ if it doesn't get enough water.

6. Have you ever told a __lie__?

7. May I have another __piece__ of paper?

8. The teacher showed a __movie__ after we talked about the city.

9. The police are looking for the __thief__ who ran out of the bank with the money.

10. I have been an aunt since my __niece__ Kris was born.

11. The team can play softball in that __field__.

12. Each knight in the painting is holding a heavy __shield__.

chief
shield
die
piece
niece
necktie
thief
lie
field
believe
movie
tie

Words containing *ie* in context   67

In some words, two vowels together stand for one vowel sound. The letters **ou** can stand for the vowel sounds you hear in **soup** and **should**.

soup
sh**ou**ld

Read the list of words. Notice the sound that **ou** stands for in each word. Write each word under the correct heading.

| group | wouldn't | could | through | coupon |
| would | shouldn't | youth | couldn't | you |

Order of words may vary.

ou as in **soup**	**ou** as in **should**
group	would
youth	wouldn't
through	shouldn't
coupon	could
you	couldn't

Read the sentences and the word choices. Circle the word that makes sense in each sentence.

1. Grandmother told me I (through, (should)) remember to wear my coat.

2. ((Wouldn't), Youth) it be nice to have a picture of that sunset?

3. We save money by using (should, (coupons)) when we shop.

4. A ((group), couldn't) of six children will play on each team.

5. Our teacher told us we (coupon, (could)) write a story.

6. What kind of (should, (soup)) do I smell cooking?

7. We will hike over the hill and (would, (through)) the woods.

68   Symbol-sound association of words containing *ou*; Words containing *ou* in context

Vowel Pairs: OU

Name

In some words, two vowels together stand for one vowel sound. The letters **ou** can stand for the vowel sounds you hear in **touch** and **doughnut**.

touch
doughnut

Read the list of words. Notice the sound that **ou** stands for in each word. Write each word under the correct heading.

| double | couple | dough | southern | shoulder |
| enough | although | young | though | |

Order of words may vary.

ou as in **touch**	**ou** as in **doughnut**
double	although
enough	dough
couple	though
young	shoulder
southern	

Read the sentences and the word choices. Circle the word that makes sense in each sentence.

1. Have you ever tasted bread ((dough), double) like this?
2. Debbie knows how to make whole wheat (double, (doughnuts)).
3. Would you like to visit my uncle in the ((country) couple)?
4. Jennie's ((cousin) though) can make flutes out of wood.
5. The player who made a ((touchdown), through) jumped up and down.
6. I put the backpack over my (southern, (shoulder)).
7. Do you have ((enough) although) wood to build a fire?

Symbol-sound association of words containing *ou*; Words containing *ou* in context

69

Vowel Pairs: OU

Name

Read the story. Circle each word that contains **ou.** Then answer the questions that follow. There are twenty-three words that contain **ou.**

Though we had never done it before, our youth group planned to make bread. We should have started with something easy, but we like bread! We went through the food store with many coupons, buying enough for an army.

Jan wanted us to get double of everything on our list. Doug had to carry a large bag of flour over his shoulder. The shopkeeper said it looked as if we were going to open a shop with all of the bread we planned to make.

The next day we all met at the home of Jan's cousin. Our plan was to first mix a little bit of the dough. We didn't have any trouble. Before long, we had baked a beautiful loaf of bread. We spent the rest of the day baking bread. By the time we were through we had enough for each of us to take a loaf home.

I shared my bread with my family. My dad said, "The group you belong to is young, but they surely know how to bake." He should know. He ate five pieces!

Use the story to answer the questions.

1. What word from the first paragraph rhymes with **dough**? _though_
2. What kind of group baked the bread? _youth_
3. What did the group take to the store in order to save money? _coupons_
4. What word from the second paragraph means "twice as much"? _double_
5. How did Doug carry the flour? _over his shoulder_
6. What word from the third paragraph means "finished"? _through_

70

Identifying words containing *ou*; Words containing *ou* in context

---

Vowel Pairs

Name

Read the list of words below. Then read the sentences that follow. Write the word from the list that makes sense in each sentence.

necktie	field	dough	would	should
chief	enough	tie	believe	
route	touch	movie	through	

1. I have never worn a _necktie_ before.
2. Will you show me how to _tie_ it?
3. What _would_ I do without your help?
4. We can make this _dough_ into bread or rolls.
5. There may be _enough_ of the mix to make both.
6. Let's taste the bread as soon as we're _through_.
7. This is the _route_ shown on the map that we should follow.
8. It will take us past a _field_ of corn.
9. Can you _believe_ that covered wagons once used this road?
10. Would you and your brother like to see a good _movie_?
11. The show is about a well-known Indian _chief_.
12. The zoo worker said that some snakes _should_ be fed every day.
13. She asked us if we'd like to _touch_ the skin of a snake.

Review of words containing vowel digraphs in context: *ie, ou*

71

Two Sounds of Y

Name

When **y** comes at the end of a word that has no other vowel, the **y** usually stands for the long-**i** sound as in **fly**.
When **y** comes at the end of a word that has another vowel, the **y** usually stands for the long-**e** sound as in **pony**.

fl**y**   pon**y**

Read the words and look at the pictures. Circle the word that tells about each picture.

fly (jelly)	spy (puppy)	carry (cry)
dry (daisy)	fly (funny)	fry (forty)
sky (snowy)	try (rainy)	funny (fry)
daisy (dry)	silly (sky)	(rocky) cry

72

Symbol-sound association of words containing *y* as a vowel

Two Sounds of Y

Read the words below. Write **long e** or **long i** next to each word to show the sound that **y** stands for.

fl**y**   pon**y**

1. fly   *long i*
2. angry   long e
3. sixty   long e
4. why   long i
5. dry   long i
6. thirsty   long e
7. stormy   long e
8. shy   long i
9. lucky   long e
10. fry   long i
11. empty   long e
12. cry   long i

Read the sentences and the word choices. Circle the word that makes sense in each sentence.

1. Tommy will (try, fry) to answer each of your questions.
2. Can you get me a (carry, copy) of the story you read to us today?
3. We can go sled riding on the first (sixty, snowy) day.
4. When I learned that my best friend was moving, I began to (dry, cry).
5. Should we buy a pack of twenty or (rainy, forty) paper plates for the party?
6. On the day we began our trip there wasn't a cloud in the (shy, sky).
7. Are those math books too (heavy, healthy) for you to carry?
8. I'd like to know (shy, why) the date of the football game was changed.

Two Sounds of Y

Read the list of words. Notice the sound that **y** stands for in each word. Write each word under the correct heading.

fl**y**   pon**y**

| try | sky | sixty | stormy | fry |
| cry | penny | rocky | shiny | shy |

Long **i** as in **fly**	Long **e** as in **pony**
try	penny
cry	sixty
sky	rocky
fry	stormy
shy	shiny

Words may be listed in any order.

Read the sentences. Complete each sentence by writing a word from the exercise above. The word you write must make sense in the sentence.

1. Would you like to ___*try*___ to fly my new kite?
2. We climbed up the steep, ___rocky___ hillside.
3. Will that school bus hold more than ___sixty___ children?
4. Have you ever tried to count each star in the ___sky___?
5. Uncle Richard can bake or ___fry___ the fish in a pan for you.
6. Aunt Janie's new ___shiny___ bicycle is silver.

PROGRESS CHECK
Vowel Pairs and Sounds of Y

Read the list of words below. Then read the sentences that follow. Write the word from the list that makes sense in each sentence.

try	taught	weight	raccoon	healthy
field	trail	cousin	cheese	straw
toast	chew	window	through	

1. We should ___try___ to get together to play basketball.
2. I would like two eggs and some ___toast___ with jam this morning.
3. The farmer carried a bale of ___straw___ into the barn.
4. The nurse always checks the baby's ___weight___ on the scales.
5. Dennis ___taught___ us how to use a rowboat.
6. What kind of ___cheese___ should I put on this sandwich?
7. Mandy's puppy likes to ___chew___ toy bones.
8. We can fly kites from the grassy ___field___.
9. Eating good food helps you stay ___healthy___.
10. I wish my ___cousin___ could go shopping with us.
11. Every year the hiking ___trail___ is used by many people.
12. I never rode ___through___ a tunnel.
13. If you look out this ___window___, you can see the lights of the city.
14. Did you see that ___raccoon___ walking on our picnic table?

Reading and Writing Wrap-Up

City Workers

Many people in the city work to help us. They do things for us that we cannot do for ourselves.

Police

Police officers help us in many ways. They help people cross the street safely. They help little children find their way if they are lost. They find people who break the law. They make our cities safe to live in.

Mail Carriers

Mail carriers bring letters and newspapers to people's homes. They also bring books, toys, and clothes that we have sent away for. They do their work in sun, snow, rain, or wind.

Fire Fighters

Fire fighters are ready at all times to fight fires. They put out fires in homes and other buildings. They save people's lives. They go to schools to teach children about fire safety.

1. Check the answer that tells the main idea.

✓ people who help us

_____ what people can do to help the police

_____ how to fight fires

2. Write two things that fire fighters do.

They put out fires. They save people's lives. They teach children

about fire safety. Other answers are also possible.

Name _____

3. Write the name of the worker under each picture.

fire fighter   police officer   mail carrier

4. In what way are a police officer and a fire fighter the same?

They both save lives. They both keep us safe. Other answers are possible.

5. Tell how your life might be different without one of these city workers.

     police   mail carriers   fire fighters

Answers will vary.

_____

_____

6. Choose one of these city workers. Tell how this person helps people in the city.

     bus driver   mayor   lifeguard   street cleaner

Answers will vary.

_____

_____

Consonant Pairs

Words to use: shelf, shield, child, thorn, whistle, chin, shop, shark, sheet

Name _____

Two consonants together can stand for one sound. Some consonants that stand for one sound are **sh, ch, th,** and **wh.** At the beginning of some words, three consonants together stand for a special sound as in **three.**

shoe   **wh**eel
chair   **thr**ee
thin

Name the pictures. Write the letters that stand for the beginning sound in each picture name.

thr ead	__s h__ ovel	__t h__ irteen
__c h__ ain	__w h__ eel	__ch__ imney

Read the sentences. Complete the unfinished word in each sentence by writing the missing letters. Choose from the following consonant pairs: **sh, ch, th, wh, thr.** You may use a consonant pair more than once.

1. My dog looks like a puppy, but he is _thr_ ee years old.

2. When he was a puppy, he would drag my old ____w h____ ite shirt around.

3. Sometimes he would hide it under a ____c h____ air.

4. Do you know that he is still afraid of his own ____s h____ adow?

5. I like to ____thr____ ow a ball for him to catch.

6. I ____t h____ ink my dog is great fun to watch!

Consonant Pairs

Name _____

Read each sentence and the words beside it. Write the word that makes sense in each sentence.

1. If you get some _thread_ , I will fix your coat.	cheese thread shed
2. I always lay my glasses on this __shelf__ .	three shelf check
3. In art class, we form clay into many different __shapes__ .	shapes change thanks
4. The police believe that a __thief__ tried to break into the bank.	thief whip chin
5. I will read my book __while__ you talk to the man who works in the children's library.	child while shield
6. Are there any sea animals bigger than a __whale__ ?	chain shake whale
7. Is there a __chance__ that you'll be able to go swimming with me?	shark than chance
8. The queen sat on a __throne__ to receive her crown.	shook throne choke
9. Our group would like to __thank__ you for your help with the play.	thank chain shadow
10. Before we build a fire, let's have the __chimney__ cleaned.	thirteen chimney whistle

---

Ending Consonant Pairs

Name _____

At the end of a word, two or three consonants together can stand for one sound. Some consonants that stand for one sound are **sh, ch, tch, th,** and **ng.**

wi**sh**   wi**th**
ea**ch**   ri**ng**
ca**tch**

Name the pictures. Write the letters that stand for the ending sound in each picture name.

pea __ch__	wa__t c h__	bru__s h__
tee__t h__	ben__c h__	stri__n g__

Read the sentences. Complete the unfinished word in each sentence by writing the letters that stand for the ending sound. Choose from the following consonant pairs: **sh, ch, tch, th, ng.** You may use a consonant pair more than once. The word you form must make sense in the sentence.

1. Please come alo__ng__ with Callie and me.

2. Bo__t h__ of us would like you to join the baseball team.

3. Today the coach will tea__c h__ us how to pitch.

4. Next week we will learn more about how to ca__t c h__ the ball.

5. We'll have to ru__s h__ if we want to be at the field on time.

Words to use: dish, such, catch, sang, fish, each, patch, bath, swing, peach, hatch, tooth

Read each sentence and the words beside it. Write the word that makes sense in each sentence.

1. The band will _march_ onto the field and play the school song.
   - match
   - math
   - march

2. This morning we bought enough _string_ for two kites.
   - scratch
   - splash
   - string

3. A large _branch_ was broken off our elm tree during the storm.
   - both
   - brush
   - branch

4. The picture will turn out better if you use a _flash_ on your camera.
   - flash
   - splash
   - crash

5. How many _teeth_ does the baby have now?
   - teach
   - teeth
   - leash

6. When the bell _rang_, the children hurried from the playground to the classroom.
   - ranch
   - rash
   - rang

7. Our sleds made a _path_ through the snowy woods.
   - path
   - patch
   - peach

8. The _switch_ on this lamp is broken.
   - switch
   - such
   - swing

9. The kitten didn't mean to _scratch_ you.
   - spring
   - scratch
   - sang

10. When I visit my cousins' farm, I like to _brush_ the horses.
    - branch
    - booth
    - brush

Words containing final consonant digraphs in context: sh, ch, tch, th, ng

81

The letters **gh** sometimes stand for the sound of **f**, as in lau**gh**. The letters **ph** usually stand for the sound of **f**, as in ele**ph**ant.

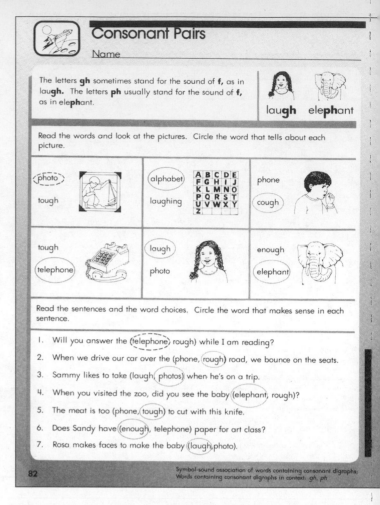

lau**gh**   ele**ph**ant

Read the words and look at the pictures. Circle the word that tells about each picture.

| (photo) tough | | (alphabet) laughing | ABCDE FGHIJ KLMNO PQRST UVWXY Z | phone (cough) |
| tough (telephone) | | (laugh) photo | | enough (elephant) |

Read the sentences and the word choices. Circle the word that makes sense in each sentence.

1. Will you answer the (telephone, rough) while I am reading?

2. When we drive our car over the (phone, (rough)) road, we bounce on the seats.

3. Sammy likes to take (laugh, (photos)) when he's on a trip.

4. When you visited the zoo, did you see the baby ((elephant), rough)?

5. The meat is too (phone, (tough)) to cut with this knife.

6. Does Sandy have ((enough), telephone) paper for art class?

7. Rosa makes faces to make the baby ((laugh), photo).

82

Symbol-sound association of words containing consonant digraphs;
Words containing consonant digraphs in context: gh, ph

Read the list of words below. Then read the sentences that follow. Write the word from the list that makes sense in each sentence.

tough	elephant	telephone	alphabet
laugh	enough	rough	nephew
microphone	rougher	photograph	laughing

1. You may want to use a _microphone_ when you speak to large groups.

2. Will Brad have _enough_ time to visit us this week?

3. Dad is teaching Sue the letters of the _alphabet_.

4. I know you'll _laugh_ when you read this funny story.

5. Because the wood of the chair is _rough_, we'll use sandpaper to make it smooth.

6. My sister is my aunt's niece, and my brother is her _nephew_.

7. The children were _laughing_ at the circus clown.

8. I am sorry that the meat I cooked is so _tough_.

9. This road is _rougher_ than it was last winter.

10. I can't hear the _telephone_ ringing when I'm working outside.

11. Ann wants to give me a _photograph_ of her cats.

12. Val has always wanted to feed peanuts to an _elephant_.

Words containing gh and ph in context

83

Read the list of words below. Then read the clues that follow. Write the word from the list that matches each clue.

| rough | tough | laugh | telephone | photo |
| nephew | enough | alphabet | elephant | |

1. not smooth — _rough_

2. what you do when you think something is funny — _laugh_

3. a boy who has an aunt or uncle — _nephew_

4. starts with **a, b, c** — _alphabet_

5. as much as is needed — _enough_

6. something you can use to talk with another person — _telephone_

7. hard to chew or cut — _tough_

8. a picture that is taken with a camera — _photo_

9. a large circus animal — _elephant_

Read the sentences and the word choices. Circle the word that makes sense in each sentence.

1. Her little sister knows the letters of the ((alphabet), elephant).

2. Please answer the (tough, (telephone)) for me.

3. The bark of that tree feels very ((rough), laugh).

4. I would like to see the (enough, (photos)) you took with your camera.

5. The jokes in your book made me (nephew, (laugh)).

84

Words containing gh and ph; Words containing gh and ph in context

Consonant Pairs

Name _____

Read each clue. Write **sh, ch, wh, ng,** or **gh** to complete the word that matches the clue.

1. a food made from milk — __ch__eese
2. something you blow into that makes a high noise — __wh__istle
3. a tool used for digging — __sh__ovel
4. two pieces of bread with meat between them — sandwi__ch__
5. a playground toy you can sit on — swi__ng__
6. hard to cut — tou__gh__
7. something you make when you jump into water — spla__sh__

Read each clue. Write **th, ph, thr,** or **tch** to complete the word that matches the clue.

1. something that can feel sore when you have a cold — __thr__oat
2. a number greater than two — __thr__ee
3. a picture taken with a camera — __ph__oto
4. a part of your hand — __th__umb
5. a piece of cloth that covers a hole in a piece of clothing — pa__tch__
6. something that is used to make clothes — clo__th__
7. something used to light a candle — ma__tch__

Review of words containing initial and final consonant digraphs   85

Consonant Pairs

Name _____

Read each set of sentences and its list of words. Write the word from the list that makes sense in each sentence.

1. My family likes to __watch__ parades.
2. We always go early so that we can sit on a __bench__.
3. The last parade we saw had __thirty__ marching bands.
4. I clapped as I saw each one __march__ by.
5. When I knew the tunes, I would __sing__ along.
6. I was surprised to see a float being pulled by an __elephant__.
7. If I were in a parade, the children would __laugh__ at my funny clown costume.

march
laugh
thumb
watch
elephant
bench
sing
thirty
catch

1. I __wish__ this room looked nicer.
2. I wonder if I should paint the walls __white__.
3. Should I keep __both__ the lamp and the basket on that table?
4. Shall I put two or __three__ pictures on this wall?
5. Where should I hang this __shelf__ for my books?
6. Please tell me what you __think__ about this chair.
7. Did I hear you say, "Don't __change__ a thing"?

shelf
both
wish
whisper
three
white
shake
change
think

86   Assessment of words containing initial and final consonant digraphs in context

---

Vowels With *R*

Name _____

When a vowel is followed by the letter **r**, the vowel stands for a special sound that is neither long nor short. For example, **ar** stands for the sound you hear in **jar; er, ir,** and **ur** stand for the sounds you hear in **fern, bird,** and **burn; or** stands for the sound you hear in **horn.**

jar	horn
fern	burn
bird	

Name the pictures and read the sentences. Circle the word in each sentence that has the same vowel sound as the picture name.

barn — 1. This spring we'll be planting corn in our (garden).

fork — 2. Amy's brother is too (short) to see out the car window.

arm — 3. I would like to knit a (scarf) that will match the color of this skirt.

horse — 4. The kitten likes to curl up and sleep on the front (porch).

bird — 5. My friends and I put on a make-believe (circus) in the park.

jar — 6. An (artist) could turn this white wall into a beautiful picture.

turtle — 7. If you (turn) down this path, you will see a pine forest.

Sound-symbol association of words containing r-controlled vowels   87

Vowels With *R*

Name _____

Read the list of words below. Then read the questions that follow. Write the word from the list that answers each question.

turkey	porch	nurse	storm	stars
scarf	dirt	forest	slippers	herd
purple	thirty	card	ladder	

1. What is a large bird? __turkey__
2. In what is a seed planted? __dirt__
3. What brings snow or rain? __storm__
4. What can you sign and send in the mail? __card__
5. What can be worn on your feet? __slippers__
6. What can you wear to keep your head or neck warm? __scarf__
7. Who helps care for people who are ill? __nurse__
8. What can you use to climb to high places? __ladder__
9. What has many trees? __forest__
10. What is a group of cows called? __herd__
11. What can be seen in the sky at night? __stars__
12. What number comes after twenty-nine? __thirty__
13. What is a color? __purple__
14. What can be on the front of a house? __porch__

88   Words containing r-controlled vowels in context

Vowels With R

Name _____

Read the sentences and the word choices. Circle the word that makes sense in each sentence.

1. I go to the craft center with my friends each Saturday ((morning,) market).

2. The ((teachers,) torch) show us a different craft every week.

3. One time, we made little ((lanterns,) large) out of tin.

4. Another time, I used a new kind of paint to color a white ((shirt,) sharp).

5. I have made a scarf out of yarn and a belt out of (ladder, (leather)).

6. Sometimes I make mistakes, but most of my things (torn, (turn)) out all right.

7. My work at the center makes me want to become an ((artist,) other).

---

1. Last night's storm made a mess of our ((yard,) yarn).

2. Now we must try to save the plants in our (germ, (garden)).

3. Our tall green corn plants are now lying in the ((dirt,) dart).

4. I'll use a broom to sweep the front (perch, (porch)).

5. My older brother and my ((sister,) squirrel) will get the tree branches off the roof.

6. We are lucky that the storm did not (her, (hurt)) the apple tree we just planted.

7. I hope the wind doesn't blow so ((hard,) horn) in the next storm.

Vowels With R

Name _____

Read each sentence and look at the letter pairs beside it. Write one of the letter pairs to complete the unfinished word in each sentence. The word you form must make sense in the sentence.

1. We planted rows of seeds in the g_ar_den.   ar, er

2. I like to watch the dancer t_ur_n when he dances on the stage.   or, ur

3. The tail of the squ_ir_rel is bushy.   ar, ir

4. Before it snows, we will cov_er_ the plants in our garden.   or, er

5. A sales cl_er_k will be able to help you find a shirt in your size.   er, or

6. We put our bikes in the shed when it began to st_or_m.   ur, or

7. I feed my t_ur_tle once a day in the morning.   or, ur

8. There are seats for f_or_ty children in the classroom.   ir, or

9. We buy our eggs and milk at a f_ar_m.   or, ar

10. You'll find the answ_er_ to your question in this book.   or, er

11. Shane would like to try out for a p_ar_t in the play.   ir, ar

12. The hamm_er_ hit my thumb instead of the nail.   er, ar

13. This ch_ar_t shows how far I have run this spring.   ar, or

14. Carla has my comb in her p_ur_se.   ar, ur

15. The group must form a c_ir_cle before the game begins.   ar, ir

---

Vowels With R

Name _____

Read the sentences and the list of words. Write the word from the list that makes sense in each sentence.

1. A _turtle_ is a good pet to keep in a small home.

2. There are twelve fresh eggs in the ___carton___.

3. The balloon made a loud noise when it ___burst___.

4. That pile of ___dirt___ must be moved before the building begins.

5. The artist uses gold and ___silver___ to make bracelets.

6. My baby brother is too ___short___ to reach the doorknob.

7. Which runner do you think will be the ___first___ to cross the finish line?

8. Please pass the salt and ___pepper___ shakers to me.

9. What kind of wood will ___burn___ best in a fireplace?

10. Sometimes my dog ___barks___ when I won't let her come outside with me.

11. Our class will hear a ___speaker___ talk about her trip to Spain.

12. My older sister lives in an ___apartment___ near our house.

13. I know spring is near when I hear the birds ___chirp___.

14. The puppy was ___born___ three weeks ago.

burn
first
chirp
pepper
silver
apartment
dirt
burst
speaker
born
turtle
barks
short
carton

Vowels With R

Name _____

Read the list of words below. Then read the sentences that follow. Write the word from the list that makes sense in each sentence.

porch	better	squirrels	thirty
hurry	alarm	slippers	birthday
parking	forget	horse	hurt

1. After school I come home and sit on the front _porch_.

2. I like to watch the ___squirrels___ run through the trees.

3. They make me ___forget___ the cares of my day.

4. Don takes lessons to learn how to ride a ___horse___.

5. His teacher says that Don's riding is getting ___better___ every week.

6. I'll be going to Kate's surprise ___birthday___ party next week.

7. The party will be held at the park behind the school ___parking___ lot.

8. I must ___hurry___ to get to the post office.

9. The mail will be picked up there in ___thirty___ minutes.

10. I jumped out of bed when the ___alarm___ rang this morning.

11. One of my ___slippers___ fell off as I ran down the hallway.

12. I'm surprised I didn't ___hurt___ myself as I hurried through the house.

OI, OY, OU, and OW

Name _____

The letters **oi** and **oy** stand for the vowel sounds in **coin** and **toys**. The letters **ou** and **ow** often stand for the vowel sounds you hear in **cloud** and **cow**.

co**i**n	cl**ou**d
to**y**s	c**ow**

Read the list of words below. Then look at the pictures. Write a word from the list that tells about each picture.

cloud   point   frown   boy   boil   bounce

cloud   boy   point

hoil   hounce   frown

Read the sentences and the word choices. Circle the word that makes sense in each sentence.

1. Last weekend my cousin and I were looking (around, allow) his basement.

2. We (foil, found) a trunk that was full of old picture books.

3. One book had a picture of a different circus (cloud, clown) on each page.

4. Another book had drawings of beautiful (flowers, found).

5. My cousin's mother told me I could have my (crowd, choice) of the old books.

6. I (join, enjoy) looking at the book about animals that I took home.

OI, OY, OU, and OW

Name _____

Read each sentence and the words beside it. Write the word that makes sense in each sentence.

1. My neighbor's little *boy* likes to ride his bicycle on the bike path.
   boil
   boy

2. My sister can name the different kinds of ___clouds___ in the sky.
   clouds
   coins

3. Every child in that family has a beautiful singing ___voice___.
   voice
   vow

4. The ___royal___ princess told the children a story.
   royal
   round

5. We learned that some plants can have ___poison___ in them.
   pound
   poison

6. Rose tries to see how high the basketball will ___bounce___.
   boiling
   bounce

7. I would like to take a picture of the sand castle before the waves ___destroy___ it.
   down
   destroy

8. Is this dark ___soil___ good for growing corn?
   scout
   soil

9. When we walked through the barn, I saw a ___mouse___ run across the floor.
   mouse
   mouth

10. The young girl ___frowned___ when she lost her balloon.
   frowned
   found

OI, OY, OU, and OW

Name _____

Read the clues and the list of words. Write the word from the list that matches each clue.

1. something that helps to keep machines running   *oil*

2. sounds   noises

3. to yell   shout

4. a large bird   owl

5. a farm tool that loosens dirt   plow

6. things that children play with   toys

7. a group of many people   crowd

8. to hit with a hammer   pound

9. something that water does when it is very hot   boils

10. dirt   soil

11. the sharp end of something   point

12. the part of the face used to smile   mouth

13. a very tall building   tower

14. a young man   boy

15. a sea animal that lives in a shell   oyster

pound
oil
shout
tower
plow
soil
noises
point
boy
toys
boils
crowd
mouth
owl
oyster

OI, OY, OU, and OW

Name _____

Read each sentence and look at the letter pairs beside it. Write one of the letter pairs to complete the unfinished word in each sentence. The word you form must make sense in the sentence.

1. I will see if Dad will all__ow__ me to take the bus.   ow, oi

2. I would like to ride to t__ow__n with my friend Beth.   oy, ow

3. If we go right after school, there will be no cr__ow__ds in the stores.   ow, oy

4. Beth knows how to get ar__ou__nd from one place to another.   ou, oi

5. She will help me find a t__oy__ for Timmy's birthday.   oy, ou

6. We will go to a shop that sells stamps and c__oi__ns.   ow, oi

7. Beth thinks I will enj__oy__ looking in the other store windows, too.   ou, oy

8. We are planning to return to Beth's h__ou__se before it gets dark.   oi, ou

1. Last spring I wanted to j__oi__n an outdoors club.   oi, ow

2. My friend Joy told me about being a sc__ou__t.   oi, ou

3. I would enj__oy__ being a member of the group.   oy, ou

4. Our hike up Snowball M__ou__ntain was one I'll never forget.   ou, oi

5. The hike back d__ow__n to our campsite was not easy because the mountain paths are steep.   oi, ow

6. I am pr__ou__d to be a part of the group.   ou, oi

OI, OY, OU, and OW

Name _____

Read the sentences and the word choices. Circle the word that makes sense in each sentence.

1. Flowers will grow well in this rich (sound, (soil)).
2. The singer works hard to make his ((voice) choice) sound better.
3. When I went shopping, I bought eggs, milk, and a bag of (frown, (flour)).
4. Martha and Sandra are building a tall ((tower), powder) of blocks.
5. The princess doll wears a golden (count, (crown)) on her head.
6. I like to ((bounce), bow) the ball when I am on the school playground.
7. I have learned how to check the (out, (oil)) in our family car.
8. What kind of bath ((toys), town) do babies like best?
9. When you are so far away, I can hear you only if you (shower, (shout)).
10. My dog will (ground, (growl)) if he hears a strange noise.
11. The scientist can check for ((poisons), pound) in a plant.
12. I saw an (oil, (oyster)) shell when I visited the beach.
13. An older friend taught me how to ((pound), powder) a nail into a board.
14. The beautiful horses belong to the queen and her ((royal), voice) family.
15. The white, fluffy (clown, (clouds)) look pretty in the blue sky.
16. She has lived in this ((town), toy) since she was a young girl.
17. A little gray (mouth, (mouse)) ran across the barn.
18. Put the corn into the pan after the water begins to ((boil), bow).

Review of words containing diphthongs in context: oi, oy, ou, ow   97

OI, OY, OU, and OW

Name _____

Read the list of words below. Then read the sentences that follow. Write the word from the list that makes sense in each sentence.

ouch	clown	point	pound
frowning	boil	out	towel
boys	enjoy	join	choice

1. Let me know when the water in the pan starts to _____ *boil*
2. I have more than one _____ pound _____ of green beans to cook.
3. My family will _____ enjoy _____ eating something from our garden.
4. Do you know why I am _____ frowning _____?
5. I just fell _____ out _____ of that small oak tree.
6. I am not hurt, but I did yell "_____ ouch _____" when I landed.
7. My sister has fun when she dresses up as a _____ clown _____
8. She says it's fun to make girls and _____ boys _____ smile.
9. Please _____ point _____ to the row you would like to sit in.
10. Today you can have your _____ choice _____ of seats.
11. Will you _____ join _____ me when I go to the beach to swim?
12. Don't forget your sunglasses and a _____ towel _____

98   Assessment of words containing diphthongs in context: oi, oy, ou, ow

---

Endings: -ED and -ING

Words to use: call, mop, work, slip, look, color, jump, rip, help, bat, bark, clap, shop

Name _____

Many new words can be formed by adding **-ed** or **-ing** to other words. When a word ends with one vowel followed by one consonant, double the consonant before adding **-ed** or **-ing.**

| walk | walk**ing** |
| snap | snap**ped** |

Read the words and add **-ed** and **-ing** to each one. Write the new words in the blanks.

		Add **-ed**	Add **-ing**
1.	mail	*mailed*	mailing
2.	hop	hopped	hopping
3.	plant	planted	planting
4.	talk	talked	talking
5.	chip	chipped	chipping

Read the list of words below. Then read each sentence that follows. Add **-ed** or **-ing** to one of the list words to complete each sentence. Write the word in the blank. The word you form must make sense in the sentence.

thank   ask   bag   stop   sweep

1. Star _____ *asked* _____ me to help her with some yard work.
2. We began by _____ sweeping _____ the leaves into piles.
3. Then we _____ bagged _____ the leaves.
4. Star and I _____ stopped _____ when it became too dark to work.
5. Star's dad _____ thanked _____ me for my help.

Adding -ed and -ing to verbs in isolation and in context   99

Endings: -ED and -ING

Name _____

Many new words can be formed by adding **-ed** or **-ing** to other words. When a word ends in **e**, drop the **e** before adding **-ed** or **-ing.** When a word ends in a consonant followed by **y**, change **y** to **i** before adding **-ed.** Do not change **y** to **i** before adding **-ing** to a word that ends in **y.**

save	sav**ing**
hurry	hurr**ied**
carry	carry**ing**

Read the words and add **-ed** and **-ing** to each one. Write the new words in the blanks.

		Add **-ed**	Add **-ing**
1.	taste	*tasted*	tasting
2.	cry	cried	crying
3.	wave	waved	waving
4.	hope	hoped	hoping
5.	marry	married	marrying

Read the list of words below. Then read each sentence that follows. Add **-ed** or **-ing** to one of the list words to complete each sentence. Write the word in the blank. The word you form must make sense in the sentence.

shine   try   race   carry   skate

1. Yoko hit the ball and _____ *raced* _____ toward first base.
2. My friends _____ tried _____ to play softball in the rain.
3. The dog is _____ carrying _____ a stick in its mouth.
4. Have you ever _____ skated _____ on that frozen pond?
5. I can't see because the light is _____ shining _____ in my eyes.

100   Adding -ed and -ing to verbs in isolation and in context

Endings: -S and -ES

Name _____

Often new words can be formed by adding **-s** or **-es** to other words. To change many words, add the letter **-s**. When a word ends in a consonant followed by **y**, change the **y** to **i** and add **-es**.

laugh	laugh**s**
marry	marr**ies**

Read the words and add **-s** or **-es** to each one. Write the new words in the blanks.

1. draw   *draws*
2. copy   copies
3. study   studies
4. sing   sings
5. walk   walks
6. hurry   hurries

Read the list of words below. Then read each sentence that follows. Add **-s** or **-es** to one of the list words to complete each sentence. The word you form must make sense in the sentence.

listen   need   like   try   help   study   make

1. My friend Marcos _____*likes*_____ to keep busy.
2. Before Marcos goes to school, he _____makes_____ his lunch for the next day.
3. He _____listens_____ carefully to his teacher.
4. After school he _____helps_____ young children learn to swim.
5. Marcos _____tries_____ his best to get to all of his little sister's baseball games.
6. When he gets home, Marcos does his homework and _____studies_____ for his tests.
7. I think Marcos _____needs_____ much longer days.

Endings: -ES

Name _____

Many new words can be formed by adding **-es** to other words. When a word ends in **s, ss, sh, ch,** or **x,** add **-es.**

bus	bus**es**	pitch	pitch**es**
miss	miss**es**	mix	mix**es**
fish	fish**es**		

Read the words. Underline the **s, ss, sh, ch,** or **x** if it comes at the end of a word. Then add **-es** to these words. Write the new words in the blanks.

1. coach   *coaches*
2. reach   reaches
3. push   pushes
4. pass   passes
5. dress   dresses
6. wax   waxes

Read the sentences and the list of words. Add **-es** to one of the list words to complete each sentence. Write the word in the blank. The word you form must make sense in the sentence.

1. After school each child _____*dresses*_____ in play clothes.
2. Everyone _____rushes_____ to Mrs. Bello's backyard.
3. The scout leader _____teaches_____ children about camping.
4. James _____passes_____ his test when he ties the knots.
5. He _____wishes_____ that he could spend the night at the lake.
6. Alma _____brushes_____ the dirt from her backpack.
7. She pitches a tent while Tony _____watches_____ every step.
8. Using the campfire, Lin _____fixes_____ a snack.

teach
dress
rush
watch
pass
fix
wish
brush

Base Words and Endings

Name _____

A word to which an ending can be added is called a base word.   **reach**es

Read each word and write its base word in the blank.

1. closing   *close*
2. knowing   know
3. skipped   skip
4. batting   bat
5. standing   stand
6. makes   make
7. dried   dry
8. skating   skate
9. stepped   step
10. misses   miss
11. tasted   taste
12. copies   copy

Read the list of base words below. Then read each sentence that follows. Complete the sentence by adding the ending shown beside the sentence to a word from the list. Write the new word in the blank.

bake   talk   try   run   find   fish

1. One day we were _____*talking*_____ about ways that we have fun.   -ing
2. Andrew told us he _____fishes_____ in a pond near his home.   -es
3. Molly said she _____finds_____ seashells on the beach.   -s
4. Jim _____tried_____ to explain a guessing game he likes.   -ed
5. Allen said he likes _____running_____ in a race more than anything else.   -ing
6. Jessie told how she had a lot of fun when she _____baked_____ bread for her friends.   -ed

---

Endings: -ER and -EST

Name _____

In many words, the ending **-er** means "more." It can be used to compare two things. The ending **-est** means "most." It can be used to compare three or more things.

deep	deep**er**
deep	deep**est**

Read the sentences and the word choices. Circle the word that makes sense in each sentence.

1. This year's dog show should be ((greater), greatest) than last year's show.
2. There will be a race to see which of the many dogs can run (faster, (fastest)).
3. Seth hopes that his dog is ((quicker), quickest) than his cousin's dog.
4. A prize will be given to the (smaller, (smallest)) of all the dogs.
5. The (younger, (youngest)) dog of all might be one of Spot's puppies.
6. My dog may be the (older, (oldest)) dog there, but she is also the best dog in the show!

Read each sentence and the word beside it. Add **-er** or **-est** to the word to complete the sentence. Write the new word in the blank. The word you form must make sense in the sentence.

1. I must be the _____*slowest*_____ shopper in this town.   slow
2. To save money, I try to find the _____lowest_____ of all the prices.   low
3. Because I am _____taller_____ than I was last year, I must buy some new clothes.   tall
4. My dad says I might have to buy the _____highest_____ priced pants in the store.   high
5. I guess I take a _____longer_____ time choosing my things than you do.   long

Many new words can be formed by adding **-er** or **-est** to other words. When a word ends with one vowel followed by one consonant, double the consonant before adding **-er** or **-est**. When a word ends in **e**, drop the **e** before adding **-er** or **-est**. When a word ends in a consonant followed by **y**, change the **y** to **i** before adding **-er** or **-est**.

wet	wet**test**
wise	wis**er**
cloudy	cloud**ier**

Add **-er** and **-est** to each word below. Write the new words in the blanks.

		Add **-er**	Add **-est**
1.	busy	busier	busiest
2.	big	bigger	biggest
3.	sunny	sunnier	sunniest
4.	late	later	latest
5.	light	lighter	lightest

Read each sentence and the word beside it. Add **-er** or **-est** to the word to complete the sentence. Write the new word in the blank. The word you form must make sense in the sentence.

1. Lance's shop has the _cutest_ stuffed toys I've seen. cute
2. The orange cat is _fatter_ than my yellow cat. fat
3. That clown has the _funniest_ hat that I've seen. funny
4. You'd like seeing the deer that is _taller_ than a person. tall
5. The shop has the _finest_ toys of any store in town. fine

Read each sentence and the word shown below the blank. Add **-er** or **-est** to the word to complete the sentence. Write the new word in the blank.

1. This book is _sillier_ than the book about the pink turtle. (silly)
2. Will the stove get _hotter_ than it is now? (hot)
3. Can you make this room look _neater_ than it looked before? (neat)
4. Please buy the _brightest_ poster you can find. (bright)
5. Is that the _biggest_ of all the hot-air balloons in the show? (big)
6. Where can I buy the _nicest_ flowers in town? (nice)
7. The day of the school play is our _busiest_ day of the year. (busy)
8. This metal ring is _looser_ than the wooden ring I used to have. (loose)
9. Ellen's apartment is _closer_ to the school than mine is. (close)
10. The baby looked _happier_ after she took her nap. (happy)
11. Brenda's dog is _fatter_ than Ken's dog. (fat)

Read the list of words below. Then read each sentence that follows. Complete the sentence by adding one of the endings shown beside the sentence to a word from the list. Write the new word in the blank. The word you form must make sense in the sentence.

fish   bat   chase   study   jump   bake

1. Tim's father _bakes_ bread in the new oven. -s, -es
2. Peggy _fishes_ for trout in a stream near the park. -s, -es
3. Will you be _batting_ in the next baseball game? -ed, -ing
4. Len _studies_ his spelling words each morning. -es, -ing
5. Elena _jumped_ into the swimming pool from the diving board. -ed, -ing
6. Today I _chased_ my kitten around the house. -ed, -ing

Add **-er** and **-est** to each word below. Write the new words in the blanks.

		Add **-er**	Add **-est**
1.	slow	slower	slowest
2.	sad	sadder	saddest
3.	fine	finer	finest
4.	pretty	prettier	prettiest
5.	large	larger	largest
6.	loud	louder	loudest

A word that stands for one of something is a singular word. A word that stands for two or more of something is a plural word. To write the plural form of most words, add **-s.** To form the plural of a word that ends in **s, ss, sh, ch,** or **x,** add **-es.** To form the plural of a word that ends in a consonant followed by **y,** change the **y** to **i** and add **-es.**

toy	toy**s**
lunch	lunch**es**
baby	bab**ies**

Read the words. Write the plural form of each one.

1.	shoe	shoes	5.	boss	bosses
2.	watch	watches	6.	room	rooms
3.	brush	brushes	7.	puppy	puppies
4.	party	parties	8.	fox	foxes

Read the sentences and the list of words. Write the plural form of a word from the list to complete each sentence. The word you form must make sense in the sentence.

1. We can ride our _bikes_ to the market.
2. Let's go after we eat and do the _dishes_.
3. Eva wants us to buy some _daisies_ that can be planted.
4. She will plant them in the ground in straight _rows_.
5. We can pay for the flowers with five dollars and some _pennies_.
6. We will ask for _boxes_ to hold the daisies we buy.

row
box
dish
six
bike
penny
daisy
story

Plurals: Changing *F* to *V*

Name _____

Words to use: elf, life, wife, loaf, knife, calf, half

To write the plural form of most words that end in **f** or **fe**, change the **f** or **fe** to **v** and add **-es**.	leaf	lea**ves**
	life	li**ves**

Read each sentence and the words beside it. Write the plural form of one of the words to complete each sentence. The word you form must make sense in the sentence.

1. The cook uses sharp _knives_ to cut the meat.
   life
   knife

2. How many _loaves_ of bread are needed to make forty sandwiches?
   loaf
   leaf

3. In this make-believe story, a group of _elves_ makes a family very happy.
   shelf
   elf

4. Most of those _calves_ were born last week.
   calf
   half

5. The tree grows new _leaves_ each spring.
   leaf
   life

6. This book tells about the _lives_ of well-known men and women.
   life
   loaf

7. In the play, a bank was robbed by two _thieves_.
   thief
   knife

8. My brother and sister learned how to build _shelves_ for their books.
   shelf
   self

Irregular Plurals

Name _____

Words to use: man, tooth, child, mouse, woman, goose, foot, sheep

The plurals of some words are formed by changing the spelling of their singular forms.

child - children	man - men	woman - women
tooth - teeth	foot - feet	mouse - mice
goose - geese		

The plural forms of some words can be the same as their singular forms.

sheep   deer   fish

Read each set of sentences and its list of words. Write the plural form of a word from the list to complete each sentence. The word you form must make sense in the sentence.

1. _Children_ will enjoy seeing the puppet show.
   man
   fish
2. How much wool can you get from six _sheep_?
   Child
3. I have seen _geese_ flying over our campsite.
   foot
4. Many women and _men_ will vote tomorrow.
   goose
5. I found a nest of baby _mice_ that were each smaller than my thumb.
   sheep
   mouse

1. Every morning, Dad asks me if I have brushed my _teeth_.
   fish
2. We need more men and _women_ to drive the school buses.
   woman
   deer
3. If we wait near the woods, we might see some _deer_ (deers is also acceptable).
   tooth
   child
4. The new shoes I am wearing make my _feet_ hurt.
   foot
5. Joy came home carrying a pail filled with _fish_ (fishes is also acceptable) that she caught at the lake.
   mouse

Plurals

Name _____

Words to use: key, song, bench, boss, elf, life, glove, brush, wife, candle, lunch, loaf, dollar, jelly, knife, neighbor, bunny, fish, mountain, puppy, sheep, fox, party, goose

Read the paragraphs and the list of words. Write the plural form of a word from the list to complete each sentence. The words you form must make sense in the paragraph.

I think you will like this store better than the _stores_ we shopped in before. It is full of things for _children_ under the age of twelve. The clothing part of the store has jeans, shirts, and _dresses_. Another part of the store has _watches_ to tell time, as well as rings and bracelets.

Most children like to look at the toys. They are in the biggest part of the store. The _shelves_ are full of every kind of toy. There are dolls that look like newborn _babies_, and dolls that are dressed like grown men and _women_. I have seen sets of _dishes_ you could eat from and small sinks and stoves. There are also toy foods, such as apples and _peaches_.

You might like seeing the stuffed animals like those puppies and _calves_. I never leave the store without looking at the _games_ that can be played by one or more players. You can see why I save my _pennies_ before I visit this store!

watch
baby
calf
store
peach
shelf
dress
dish
penny
child
game
woman

Showing Ownership

Name _____

To make most words show ownership, add an apostrophe (') and **s**. In the example, **dog's bone**, the **'s** shows that the bone belongs to the dog.	dog**'s** bone

Rewrite each group of words below, adding **'s** to form words that show ownership.

1. the horse that Bruce owns   _Bruce's horse_
2. the sock that the baby wears   _baby's sock_
3. the windows of a truck   _truck's windows_
4. the backpack that Sal owns   _Sal's backpack_
5. the game that belongs to Kim   _Kim's game_
6. the paw of a cat   _cat's paw_

Read each sentence and the words beside it. Add **'s** to one of the words to complete the sentence. The word you form must make sense in the sentence.

1. The _bank's_ doors open each day at nine o'clock.
   bank
   book

2. My _aunt's_ office is in the center of the town.
   apple
   aunt

3. Her _father's_ speech was heard by many people.
   father
   farm

4. The _bush's_ flowers are light pink.
   brush
   bush

5. My math _teacher's_ writing is easy to read.
   teacher
   tractor

Showing Ownership

Name _____

To make a singular word show ownership, add an apostrophe (') and **s.** To make a plural word that ends in **s** show ownership, add just an apostrophe. In the examples, **'s** shows that the bones belong to one dog, and **s'** shows that the bones belong to more than one dog.

dog**'s** bones
dogs**'** bones

Read the words and look at the pictures. Circle the words that tell about each picture.

girl's gloves	tree's bark	truck's wheels
(girls' gloves)	(trees' bark)	(trucks' wheels)
dog's food	boy's photos	skunk's stripes
(dogs' food)	(boys' photos)	(skunks' stripes)

Rewrite each group of words below, adding ' or 's to the underlined word to show ownership.

1. the wings of the <u>birds</u>   *birds' wings*
2. the tent that is used by the <u>scouts</u>   scouts' tent
3. the house that belongs to a <u>teacher</u>   teacher's house
4. the office used by two <u>dentists</u>   dentists' office
5. the covers of the <u>books</u>   books' covers
6. the tail of a <u>monkey</u>   monkey's tail

Showing Ownership

Name _____

Read each sentence and the words shown below the blank. Write the word that makes sense in the sentence.

1. The ___ *dog's* ___ tail is short and brown.
   (dog's, dogs')
2. The two ___ trucks' ___ steering wheels are the same color.
   (truck's, trucks')
3. That ___ flag's ___ stripes are green and white.
   (flag's, flags')
4. The ___ boys' ___ birthdays are on the same day.
   (boy's, boys')
5. Did you see ___ Mary's ___ new puppy?
   (Marys', Mary's)
6. I could see the ___ cats' ___ heads through the little window.
   (cat's, cats')
7. My youngest ___ sister's ___ blocks are on her bedroom floor.
   (sister's, sisters')
8. We found ___ Mother's ___ hammer under the steps.
   (Mother's, Mothers')
9. The ___ kitten's ___ coat is always kept clean.
   (kittens', kitten's)
10. The ___ rooms' ___ floors are made of wood.
    (room's, rooms')
11. My ___ friend's ___ nose was sunburned yesterday.
    (friend's, friends')
12. The ___ cars' ___ engines were made in this city.
    (car's, cars')

Plurals and Showing Ownership

Name _____

Read the words and write the plural form of each one.

1. bicycle   *bicycles*
2. wolf   wolves
3. school   schools
4. baby   babies
5. child   children
6. box   boxes
7. apple   apples
8. party   parties
9. glass   glasses
10. man   men
11. patch   patches
12. deer   deer (deers is also acceptable)
13. elf   elves
14. puppy   puppies

Rewrite each group of words below, adding ' or 's to the underlined word to show ownership.

1. the whiskers of the <u>cats</u>   *cats' whiskers*
2. the field that is used by the <u>players</u>   players' field
3. the apartment that belongs to <u>Joan</u>   Joan's apartment
4. the library used by the <u>teachers</u>   teachers' library
5. the playground owned by the <u>school</u>   school's playground
6. the hats worn by the <u>fire fighters</u>   fire fighters' hats
7. the smile of the <u>child</u>   child's smile
8. the backpack that belongs to <u>Bob</u>   Bob's backpack

PROGRESS CHECK
Endings and Plurals

Name _____

Read each sentence and the word beside it. Complete each sentence by adding one of the endings shown below to the word. Write the new word in the blank. The word you form must make sense in the sentence.

-ed   -ing   -s   -es   -er   -est

1. A storm began while we were *playing* in the yard.   play
2. That is the ___ silliest ___ hat I have ever seen!   silly
3. A few of us ___ carried ___ the logs for the fire.   carry
4. Aunt Janet ___ thanks ___ me every time I visit.   thank
5. When Dave's football clothes are dirty, he ___ washes ___ them.   wash

Pick Up Page 116 From Teacher Annotated Edition at 45%

6. The crowd ___ clapped ___ when the show was over.   clap
7. Celina seems ___ happier ___ today than she was yesterday.   happy
8. Every afternoon a jet ___ flies ___ over our house.   fly

Read the words and write the plural form of each one.

1. brush   *brushes*
2. friend   friends
3. box   boxes
4. book   books
5. buggy   buggies
6. knife   knives
7. mouse   mice
8. city   cities
9. match   matches
10. shelf   shelves
11. sheep   sheep
12. class   classes

Showing Ownership

Name _____

Read each sentence and the words beside it. Write the word that makes sense in each sentence.

1. This spelling _____ *book's* _____ pages are ripped.	book's	books'
2. Her _____ brothers' _____ bedrooms are painted red and blue.	brother's	brothers'
3. Our many _____ trees' _____ leaves are different shades of green.	tree's	trees'
4. _____ Jack's _____ school was built last year.	Jack's	Jacks'
5. The three _____ clowns' _____ noses were shiny and red.	clown's	clowns'
6. The bedroom _____ phone's _____ ring woke me up.	phone's	phones'
7. The _____ park's _____ lawn is always green.	park's	parks'
8. All of these _____ pictures' _____ frames are made of wood and metal.	picture's	pictures'
9. The _____ elephants' _____ trunks are strong enough to carry logs.	elephant's	elephants'
10. My oldest _____ sister's _____ shoe size is a five.	sister's	sisters'

Assessment of using singular and plural possessives in context   117

Reading and Writing Wrap-Up

Name _____

The Boy Who Cried "Wolf!"

This is a story that teaches something important about life. Read to see if you can find out what it is.

Once there was a boy who looked after sheep. He had nothing to do all day but watch the sheep, and he was bored.

One day the boy thought of a way to have some fun, so he ran into the village shouting, "Wolf! Wolf! A wolf is after the sheep!"

All the people in the village left their work to help the boy. But when they reached the place where the sheep were grazing, there was no wolf in sight. The boy laughed at the people for believing his trick. The next day the boy played the same trick. Now he was having fun.

On the third day, the boy saw a hungry wolf coming near the flock, and he got very frightened. He ran as fast as his legs would carry him to the village. "Help!" he cried. "A wolf is going to kill the sheep!"

But this time the people did not leave their work to help the boy. They said, "That boy is just trying to fool us again by telling another lie." When the boy returned to the sheep, he saw that the wolf had killed them all.

The people were very angry when they found out the boy had not been telling a lie this time. They said, "People who tell lies cannot be believed even when they say something that is true."

A. Answer the following questions.
1. What was the job of the boy in the story?

The boy was a shepherd or sheep herder. He took care of sheep.

2. Why did the boy play a trick?

He was bored. He wanted to have some fun.

3. What did the people do the first time the boy played his trick?

They ran to help him.

118   Application of reading and comprehension skills in a literature context

---

Literature

Name _____

B. Check the two words in each line that have the same meaning in the story.

1. _____ play   ✓ fool   ✓ trick
2. ✓ flock   ✓ sheep   _____ grazing

C. Answer the following questions.
1. What does this story teach about life?

The story teaches that if you tell lies, no one will believe you even when you tell the truth.

2. Do you think the people were right or wrong not to believe the boy the third time he cried, "Wolf"? Tell why or why not.

Answers will vary.

_____

D. Write a story about one of the following sayings.

If you want something to be done right, do it yourself.
In time of trouble, you find out who your true friends are.
Those who harm others often end up harming themselves.

Answer will vary.

_____
_____
_____
_____
_____

Application of thinking and writing skills in a literature context   119

Compound Words

Name _____

Words to use: wishbone, highway, rainbow, snowstorm, blueberry, lifeboat, playhouse, baseball, airport, footprint, runway

A compound word is formed by joining two smaller words together. | dog + house = doghouse

Read each compound word and write the two words that form it.

1. waterfall	*water*		*fall*
2. snowflakes	snow		flakes
3. grandson	grand		son
4. bookcase	book		case
5. doorbell	door		bell
6. rainstorm	rain		storm
7. lighthouse	light		house

Read the sentences. Circle the two compound words in each sentence.

1. Can you use your (snowplow) on our (driveway)?
2. I found a (starfish) and a few (seashells) on the beach.
3. Jean will fold the (bedspread) that goes in her (bedroom).
4. My (grandfather) makes (homemade) bean soup.
5. I must have left my (raincoat) on the (playground).
6. Have you ever watched a (sunset) from the tall building (downtown)?
7. The plants will not grow (without) (sunshine).

120   Identifying words that form compound words; Identifying compound words in context

197

Compound Words

Name _____ Words to use: lighthouse, snowplow, bookcase, raincoat, rowboat, snowflake, mailbox

Read the words in each list below. Draw lines to match the words that form compound words.

book — place
rain — fall
pan — day
fire — case
birth — cakes

side — noon
snow — paper
after — walk
fire — storm
news — wood

Read the list of words below. Then read the sentences that follow. Write the word from the list that makes sense in each sentence.

notebook   cookbook   sometimes   something   oatmeal
airplane   rowboat   grandmother   airport

1. I plan to write to my *grandmother*, who lives in New York.

2. She will enjoy reading about my _____ rowboat _____ ride on the lake.

3. She may remember the time we went to the city _____ airport _____.

4. We flew in an _____ airplane _____ that took us over the town.

5. We did that because Grandmother wanted me to try _____ something _____ new.

6. She _____ sometimes _____ wants me to taste something I've never eaten before.

7. Once she tried to make me eat _____ oatmeal _____

8. As a joke, I bought her a new _____ cookbook _____ to read.

9. I could fill a _____ notebook _____ with stories about Grandmother and me!

Forming compound words. Using compound words in context   121

Compound Words

Name _____ Words to use: fireplace, birthday, snowball, sunshine, playground, driveway, homemade

Read the sentences below. Use two words from each sentence to form a compound word. Write the compound word in the blank.

1. A bird that is blue is called a *bluebird*

2. A walk near the side of a road is a _____ sidewalk

3. A cloth that covers a table is a _____ tablecloth

4. The bud of a rose is a _____ rosebud

5. A ball that is thrown through a basket is a _____ basketball

6. A brush that is used to clean each tooth is a _____ toothbrush

7. Work that is done for school is called _____ schoolwork

8. A shell that can be found near the sea is a _____ seashell

9. Corn that you can pop is called _____ popcorn

10. A bell that is near the door of a house is a _____ doorbell

11. A pot that holds tea is a _____ teapot

12. Wood that is used to build a fire is called _____ firewood

13. The print of a foot made in sand is called a _____ footprint

14. Work done at home is _____ homework

15. A tub for a bath is a _____ bathtub

16. A boat that has a sail is a _____ sailboat

122   Forming compound words in context

Contractions

Name _____ Words to use: we will (we'll), you would (you'd), are not (aren't), should not (shouldn't), I will (I'll), he is (he's), we are (we're), they have (they've), is not (isn't)

A contraction is a short way to write two words. It is written by putting two words together and leaving out a letter or letters. An apostrophe (') takes the place of the letters that are left out. The word **won't** is a special contraction made from the words **will** and **not**.

is + not = **isn't**
will + not = **won't**
we + are = **we're**
I + will = **I'll**

Read the list of contractions below. Then read the pairs of words that follow. Write a contraction from the list that stands for each word pair.

it's   she'll   weren't
we'd   hadn't   they're

1. had not   *hadn't*   4. she will   she'll

2. were not   weren't   5. we would   we'd

3. they are   they're   6. it is   it's

Read each sentence and the pair of words shown below the blank. Complete the sentence by writing the contraction that stands for the word pair.

1. Does he know that _____ *we're* _____ coming home early?
(we are)

2. Tammy _____ couldn't _____ find the letter she wrote.
(could not)

3. John _____ wasn't _____ ready to swim in the deep end of the pool.
(was not)

4. We _____ don't _____ go to school in the summer.
(do not)

5. Did you know that _____ they've _____ been visiting their friends?
(they have)

6. Ellen _____ won't _____ be able to come to our party.
(will not)

Forming contractions in isolation and in context   123

Contractions

Name _____ Words to use: I'd, they've, here's, there's, haven't, hadn't

Read the contractions below. Then write the two words for which each contraction stands.

1. wouldn't   *would not*   6. he'll   he will

2. we've   we have   7. hasn't   has not

3. didn't   did not   8. she's   she is or she has

4. that's   that is or that has   9. won't   will not

5. we'd   we would or we had   10. I've   I have

Read each sentence and the contraction shown below the blank. Complete the sentence by writing the two words for which the contraction stands.

1. _____ *I would* _____ like to move to a warmer part of the country.
(I'd)

2. It _____ does not _____ snow where you live, does it?
(doesn't)

3. _____ You have _____ not seen a snowflake since you moved there.
(You've)

4. I _____ would not _____ be able to go sled riding if I lived where you live.
(wouldn't)

5. _____ It is _____ not cold enough to go ice skating, either.
(It's)

6. _____ I am _____ not sure I want to move after all.
(I'm)

124   Identifying words that form contractions in isolation and in context

Contractions

Words to use: does not (doesn't), would not (wouldn't), will not (won't), they are (they're)

Read each sentence and find the two words in it that can be made into a contraction. Circle the two words and write the contraction in the blank.

1. The city zoo (was not) far from our school building.

   wasn't

2. It (did not) take the bus driver long to get there.

   didn't

3. Kelly and Ross (could not) wait to see the animals.

   couldn't

4. (They had) been counting the days until the trip.

   They'd

5. Kelly says that (she is) going to work in a zoo someday.

   she's

Read the sentences and the list of contractions. Write the contraction that makes sense in each sentence. The word you write must make sense in the sentence.

1. _Shouldn't_ Amy read the story to the class?

2. Jordan and Juan _weren't_ here when she read it before.

3. I think _they'll_ be sorry they missed the funny ending.

4. I told Ms. Mendes that we _should've_ made the story into a play.

5. She told us _that's_ what had been planned.

6. We can start planning after _we've_ heard the story.

they'll
that's
won't
didn't
Shouldn't
we've
weren't
should've

Forming contractions in context; Using contractions in context — 125

Compound Words and Contractions

Read the clues below. Use two words from each clue to form a compound word. Write the compound word in the blank.

1. a coat worn in the rain — _raincoat_
2. a boat that you can row — rowboat
3. a tie that is worn around the neck — necktie
4. work done around the house — housework
5. a book that tells you how to cook — cookbook
6. water from a stream that falls over a high place — waterfall(s)
7. a bell that is rung at the door of a home — doorbell

Read the word pairs below. Then write the contraction that stands for each word pair.

1. we are — _we're_
2. will not — won't
3. he will — he'll
4. you would — you'd
5. are not — aren't
6. they are — they're
7. we have — we've
8. have not — haven't
9. they have — they've
10. can not — can't
11. I am — I'm
12. she had — she'd
13. do not — don't
14. there is — there's

126 — Review of forming compound words; Forming contractions

Compound Words and Contractions

Read the list of words below. Then read the sentences that follow. Choose a word from the list to complete the compound word in each sentence. The compound word you form must make sense in the sentence.

place   port   work
case   way   room

1. I read my book and finished my home_work_
2. Each of my books is now in the book_case_
3. I took my bath and cleaned the tub in the bath_room_
4. I helped my mom build a fire in the fire_place_
5. Soon, Dad will bring my uncle home from the air_port_
6. I can't wait until I see them pull into the drive_way_

Read each sentence and the pair of words beside it. Complete each sentence with a contraction that stands for the word pair.

1. _I'll_ show you how to make paper airplanes. — I will
2. _They're_ not as hard to make as you may think. — They are
3. _Where's_ the pattern for the plane you want to make? — Where is
4. I think _you'd_ enjoy using this colored paper. — you would
5. We _haven't_ tried folding the heavier white paper. — have not
6. _Shouldn't_ we start with the smallest plane? — Should not

Assessment of forming compound words and contractions in context — 127

Prefixes: UN- and DIS-

Words to use: wrap (unwrap), opened (unopened), agree (disagree), appear (disappear), kind (unkind), dress (undress), fair (unfair), lucky (unlucky), cover (discover, uncover)

A prefix is a letter or group of letters that can be added to the beginning of a word. The prefixes **un-** and **dis-** mean "not" or "the opposite of." For example, the word **unlock** means "the opposite of lock." The word **dislike** means "not like."

un + lock = **un**lock
dis + like = **dis**like

Read the list of words below. Then read each sentence that follows. Add un- to one of the list words to complete each sentence. Write the new word in the blank. The word you form must make sense in the sentence.

safe   load   happy   lock

1. We need help to _unload_ the logs from the truck.
2. The busy street is _unsafe_ for the children who walk to school.
3. The small child looked _unhappy_ when she let go of her balloon.
4. You will need a key to _unlock_ the front door.

Read the list of words below. Then read each sentence that follows. Add dis- to one of the list words to complete each sentence. Write the new word in the blank. The word you form must make sense in the sentence.

cover   connect   agree   liked   color

1. The bright light of the sun may _discolor_ the camper's tent.
2. The scientists hope to _discover_ a cure for the illness.
3. Joey _disliked_ singing in the class play.
4. Ms. Miller will _disconnect_ the wire before she fixes the lamp.
5. Because we _disagree_, we should talk about the problem.

128 — Forming words with prefixes un- and dis-; Words containing prefixes in context

Prefixes: RE- and PRE-

Words to use: refill, preheat, retell, prepay, replace, preschool, repaid, pregame

The prefix **re-** means "again." For example, the word **refill** means "fill again." The prefix **pre-** means "before." The word **prepay** means "pay before."

re + fill = **re**fill
pre + pay = **pre**pay

Read the clues. Add **re-** or **pre-** to the underlined base word to form a word that matches the clue.

1. to wrap again _rewrap_
2. to test before _pretest_
3. to write again _rewrite_
4. to paint again _repaint_
5. to use again _reuse_
6. before a game _pregame_

Read each sentence and the words beside it. Write the word that makes sense in each sentence.

1. Ardis brought a book home from her _preschool_ class.
   retell
   preschool
   pregame

2. Do you know how to _replace_ the part on the bike?
   reread
   replay
   replace

3. The bill was _prepaid_ a week ago.
   prepaid
   pregame
   replayed

4. We watched the band march in the _pregame_ show.
   retell
   prepaid
   pregame

5. Are you able to _retell_ the tale you heard last night?
   reread
   retell
   preheat

6. Please _reread_ the story for the class.
   replace
   replay
   reread

Prefixes: OVER- and MIS-

Words to use: understand (misunderstand), judge (misjudge), bake (overbake), pay (overpay), place (misplace), lead (mislead), do (overdo), sleep (oversleep), eat (overeat)

The prefix **over-** means "too much." For example, the word **overdo** means "to do too much." The prefix **mis-** means "badly" or "wrongly." For example, the word **misuse** means "to use wrongly."

over + do = **over**do
mis + use = **mis**use

Read the list of words below. Then read each sentence that follows. Add **over-** to one of the list words to complete each sentence. Write the new word in the blank. The word you form must make sense in the sentence.

eat   sleep   cook   load   flow

1. Did you _oversleep_ on the first day of school?
2. Be careful not to _overload_ your book bag.
3. The rain made the river _overflow_.
4. The good food made me want to _overeat_.
5. If you _overcook_ the meat, it will be dry.

Read the list of words below. Then read each sentence that follows. Add **mis-** to one of the list words to complete each sentence. Write the new word in the blank. The word you form must make sense in the sentence.

understand   spell   place   treat   lead

1. If you _mistreat_ your bike, it will not run well.
2. When you _misspell_ a word, cross it out and write it correctly.
3. Did you _misunderstand_ what needed to be done?
4. If you _misplace_ your homework, you must find it or redo it.
5. That sign will _mislead_ travelers.

Prefixes

Words to use: unlock, dislike, repaint, unload, discolor, repaid, overcrowd, mistreat, misspell, overflow, unwrap, distrust, preschool, unpack, rewrap, pregame, misprint

Read each sentence and the word beside it. Add **un-**, **pre-**, or **over-** to the word to complete each sentence. Write the new word in the blank. The word you form must make sense in the sentence.

1. The _unfair_ rules were changed.   fair
2. I _prepaid_ the cost at the time I ordered.   paid
3. If you don't wake her, she will _oversleep_.   sleep
4. My dog _overeats_ when there is too much food in the dish.   eats
5. Because I lost the game, I felt _unlucky_.   lucky
6. Scott talks about his _preschool_ class.   school

Read each sentence and the word beside it. Add **dis-**, **re-**, or **mis-** to the word to complete each sentence. Write the new word in the blank. The word you form must make sense in the sentence.

1. If you _disagree_ with me, let me know.   agree
2. Grandma will _retell_ many of her stories.   tell
3. I often _misjudge_ the time when I get busy.   judge
4. I will _reheat_ the chicken soup for lunch.   heat
5. We saw the rabbit _disappear_ from sight into the red hat.   appear
6. If you _misread_ the sign, you will get lost.   read

Suffixes: -FUL and -LESS

Words to use: thought (thoughtful, thoughtless), spoon (spoonful), thank (thankful, thankless), help (helpful, helpless), cloud (cloudless), pain (painful, painless)

A suffix is a letter or group of letters that can be added to the end of a word. The suffix **-ful** usually means "full of." For example, the word **helpful** means "full of help." The suffix **-less** usually means "without." The word **hopeless** means "without hope."

help + **ful** = help**ful**
hope + **less** = hope**less**

Read the words below. Form new words by adding the suffix **-ful** or **-less** to the words. Write each word under the correct heading.

end   hand   wonder   friend   play   cloud   forget   home

Order of words may vary.

Add **-ful**	Add **-less**
handful	endless
wonderful	friendless
playful	cloudless
forgetful	homeless

Read the sentences and the list of words. Write the word from the list that makes sense in each sentence.

1. I was _careless_ when I lost my math paper.
2. Put a small _spoonful_ of salt into the soup.
3. I slept well and had a _restful_ night.
4. We are _thankful_ that we have friends like you.
5. I am glad the snake we saw is _harmless_.
6. The list of jobs to do at home seems _endless_.

careless
restful
helpful
harmless
sleepless
thankful
spoonful
endless

Suffixes: -Y and -LY

Words to use: thirsty, loudly, bumpy, quickly, nicely, dusty, sleepy, rusty, rocky, slowly

Name _____

The suffixes **-y** and **-ly** can be added to some words. For example, a day with **rain** is a **rainy** day. Something done in a **nice** way is done **nicely**.

rain + **y** = rain**y**
nice + **ly** = nice**ly**

Read the list of words below. Then read each sentence that follows. Add **-y** to one of the list words to complete each sentence. Write the new word in the blank. The word you form must make sense in the sentence.

frost   cloud   stick   luck   squeak

1. We were _____lucky_____ to get five tickets for the early show last Saturday.
2. I spilled some glue, and my desk is now _____sticky_____.
3. We didn't see much sunshine because the sky was _____cloudy_____.
4. My new boots make a _____squeaky_____ sound when I walk.
5. Because it is cold outdoors, our windows look white and _____frosty_____.

Read the list of words below. Then read each sentence that follows. Add **-ly** to one of the list words to complete each sentence. Write the new word in the blank. The word you form must make sense in the sentence.

soft   week   quick   friend   slow

1. Because he walked _____slowly_____, he missed the bus.
2. If we get dressed _____quickly_____, we can go sled riding before we eat.
3. My older brother reads a _____weekly_____ newspaper.
4. She played the song so _____softly_____ that we could hardly hear it.
5. We had fun at the party because we met some _____friendly_____ people.

Suffixes: -ABLE and -ISH

Words to use: reach (reachable), read (readable), child (childish), boy (boyish), girl (girlish), enjoy (enjoyable), wash (washable), baby (babyish)

Name _____

The suffix **-able** means "can be" or "able to be." For example, the word **washable** means "can be washed." The suffix **-ish** means "like" or "somewhat." The word **childish** means "like a child."

wash + **able** = wash**able**
child + **ish** = child**ish**

Read the words below. Form new words by adding the suffix **-able** or **-ish** to the words. Write each word under the correct heading.

yellow   baby   break   pass   girl   like   clown   change

Add **-able**	Add **-ish**
breakable	yellowish
passable	babyish
likeable	girlish
changeable	clownish

Read the sentences and the list of words. Add **-able** or **-ish** to one of the list words to complete each sentence. Write the word in the blank. The word you form must make sense in the sentence.

1. The low shelf makes the toys _____reachable_____.
2. The pond's water looks _____greenish_____.
3. It is _____foolish_____ to cross the street without looking both ways.
4. That page got wet, so the words are no longer _____readable_____.
5. You can get the stain out of a _____washable_____ shirt.

wash
green
reach
fool
read

Suffixes

Words to use: cheerful, thankful, hopeless, thoughtless, squeaky, frosty, friendly, weekly

Name _____

Read each sentence and the suffixes beside it. Add one of the suffixes to the word shown below the blank to complete the sentence. The word you form must make sense in the sentence.

1. Please speak _____loudly_____ when you give your speech.
   (loud)   -ful -ly
2. Berta has brown eyes and long, _____curly_____ brown hair.
   (curl)   -y -ful
3. After looking for my bike for an hour, I felt _____hopeless_____.
   (hope)   -less -ly
4. Pedro's _____clownish_____ act was really funny.
   (clown)   -ly -ish
5. The sun was shining, and the sky was _____cloudless_____.
   (cloud)   -less -ful
6. I can help you put some oil on this _____squeaky_____ door.
   (squeak)   -y -ly
7. The children watching the puppet show looked _____cheerful_____.
   (cheer)   -ish -ful
8. Billy is _____friendly_____ to all of his team members.
   (friend)   -ly -able
9. I will be _____truthful_____ and tell you how I feel.
   (truth)   -ful -less
10. Marta's new sweater is _____washable_____.
   (wash)   -less -able

Prefixes and Suffixes

REVIEW

Name _____

Read the clues. Add one of the prefixes or suffixes from the list to each underlined base word to form a word that matches the clue.

1. full of truth _____truthful_____
2. having frost _____frosty_____
3. the opposite of agree _____disagree_____
4. to write again _____rewrite_____
5. the opposite of trust _____distrust_____
6. to pay before _____prepay_____
7. without pain _____painless_____
8. full of care _____careful_____

pre-
dis-
re-
-ful
-less
-y

1. to do too much _____overdo_____
2. not true _____untrue_____
3. like a child _____childish_____
4. read wrongly _____misread_____
5. every week _____weekly_____
6. able to change _____changeable_____
7. to sleep too much _____oversleep_____
8. not hurt _____unhurt_____

un-
over-
mis-
-ly
-able
-ish

Prefixes and Suffixes

Name

Read the list of words below. Circle the prefix or suffix in each word.

thought(ful)	thank(less)	read(able)	(mis)treat
green(ish)	(dis)connect	fair(ly)	(un)safe
(over)flow	(re)place	(pre)heat	rust(y)

Read the list of words below. Then read the sentences that follow. Write the word from the list that makes sense in each sentence.

unpack	helpless	disappear	rewrap	restful	misplace
rocky	overload	pregame	neatly	grayish	breakable

1. The book about magic tricks shows you how to make a ball _disappear_

2. There will be a ___pregame___ show on the football field.

3. When Bill gets home, he will ___unpack___ his suitcases.

4. Please ___rewrap___ the leftover food and put it in the freezer.

5. We felt ___helpless___ when we couldn't fix the car.

6. Climbing up the ___rocky___ hillside took us most of the day.

7. Did you ___misplace___ the books you brought home?

8. I will be careful when I wash the ___breakable___ vase.

9. My new cat has a ___grayish___ coat and white paws.

10. Because I felt ill, I was told to have a ___restful___ day at home.

11. The books and papers are stacked ___neatly___ on the shelves.

12. The truck will not run well if you ___overload___ it.

Syllables

Name
Words to use: afternoon, always, begin, country, bottom, chipmunk, hungry, everyone, bark, library, move, summer, elephant, friendly, kitchen, telephone

Many words are made of small parts called syllables. Because each syllable has one vowel sound, a word has as many syllables as it has vowel sounds. The word **stone** has one vowel sound, so it has one syllable. The word **raincoat** has two vowel sounds, so it has two syllables.

Name the pictures. Write the number of syllables you hear in each picture name.

garden 2	popcorn 2	button 2
kitchen 2	cage 1	ladder 2
pineapple 3	puppet 2	log 1
soap 1	butterfly 3	sixty 2

Syllables

Name
Words to use: suntan, footprint, mailbox, bookcase, firewood, grandson, workbook, highway, bedspread, raincoat, necktie, seashell, pancakes, sunshine, airport, bluebird, airplane

A compound word should be divided into syllables between the words that make it compound.

rain/bow

Read the words below. Circle each compound word. Then write each compound word and draw a line between its syllables.

1. (sunset) _sun/set_
2. summer _____
3. (someone) some/one
4. (lighthouse) light/house
5. trouble _____
6. (notebook) note/book
7. (highway) high/way
8. jumping _____
9. broom _____
10. (railroad) rail/road
11. (starfish) star/fish
12. spray _____
13. (doghouse) dog/house
14. (baseball) base/ball
15. (homemade) home/made
16. puppy _____
17. (without) with/out
18. (bedroom) bed/room
19. (teapot) tea/pot
20. (birthday) birth/day
21. (toothbrush) tooth/brush
22. (raindrop) rain/drop
23. (lifeboat) life/boat
24. (sidewalk) side/walk
25. (snowflake) snow/flake
26. throat _____
27. (downtown) down/town
28. father _____

Syllables

Name
Words to use: unfair, rewrap, preheat, hopeless, quickly, undo, replace, overlook, overload, mistreat, misplace, reachable, yellowish, girlish, washable, oversleep, untrue, unzip, repaid

A word that has a prefix or suffix can be divided into syllables between the prefix or suffix and the base word.

un/tie
dark/ness

Read the list of words and the sentences. Divide each list word into syllables by drawing a line between the syllables. Then write the word from the list that makes sense in each sentence.

un/tie
pre/test
sleep/less
thought/ful
re/fill
dis/like
neat/ly
soft/ly
re/write
rain/y

1. Today I will _rewrite_ my story with a pen.

2. We will ___refill___ the car's gas tank before we start on our trip.

3. Please help me ___untie___ this string so I can open the box.

4. I will sing the song ___softly___ to the baby.

5. Before he started the lesson, the teacher gave us a ___pretest___ to see what we knew.

6. Calling me on my birthday was a ___thoughtful___ thing for you to do.

7. Because the dog barked for many hours, I had a ___sleepless___ night.

8. I ___dislike___ walking to school on rainy days.

9. It is hard to ride a bike on a ___rainy___ day.

10. All of the books were ___neatly___ placed on the shelves.

Syllables

Name

Words to use: walnut, border, circus, harbor, lantern, slippers, timber, normal, tunnel, sister, plaster, mitten, picnic, public, helmet, window, signal, yellow, target, center

When a word has two consonants between two vowels, the word is usually divided between the two consonants.

mon/key	cir/cus
VC/CV	VC/CV

Read the list of words. Write each word and draw a line between its syllables.

1. magnet   *mag/net*
2. blanket   blan/ket
3. harvest   har/vest
4. lumber   lum/ber
5. butter   but/ter
6. corner   cor/ner
7. mistake   mis/take
8. happen   hap/pen
9. basket   bas/ket
10. dentist   den/tist

Read each sentence and the words below each blank. Complete each sentence by writing the word that has the VC/CV pattern. Draw a line between its syllables.

1. Last *win/ter* we went to see Grandmother and Grandfather.
(weekend, winter)
2. We can buy food for the picnic at the mar/ket.
(market, store)
3. Did you leave a pen/cil on my desk this morning?
(paper, pencil)
4. The prin/cess sometimes wears a fancy crown.
(lady, princess)
5. Place a nap/kin next to each plate on the table.
(napkin, fork)
6. The baby held a sil/ver spoon in her hand.
(tiny, silver)

Syllables

Name

Words to use: nature, ivy, pony, dragon, visit, model, clever, metal, magic, unite, pedal, closet, tiny, damage, never, agent, cozy, shiver, vacant, clever, human, label, motel, camel

Words that have one consonant between two vowels can be divided into syllables in two ways. When you see a word that has one consonant between two vowels, say the word. If the first vowel sound is long, divide the word after the first vowel. If the first vowel sound is short, divide the word after the consonant that follows the vowel.

1	ē/ven	pā/per
	V/CV	V/CV
2	vĭs/it	mĕt/al
	VC/V	VC/V

Read the list of words. Write each word. Mark the first vowel of the word with ˘ if it stands for the short sound or ¯ if it stands for the long sound. Then draw a line between its syllables.

1. label   *lā/bel*
2. moment   mō/ment
3. cabin   căb/in
4. lemon   lĕm/on
5. travel   trăv/el
6. music   mū/sic
7. open   ō/pen
8. salad   săl/ad
9. robin   rŏb/in
10. silent   sī/lent
11. pupil   pū/pil
12. petal   pĕt/al
13. fever   fē/ver
14. planet   plăn/et
15. finish   fĭn/ish
16. famous   fā/mous
17. siren   sī/ren
18. pedal   pĕd/al
19. tiger   tī/ger
20. wagon   wăg/on

Syllables

Name

Words to use: legal, dragon, river, melon, climate, moment, wagon, famous, travel

Read the list of words. Write each word and draw a line between its syllables. Mark the first vowel of the word with ˘ if it stands for the short sound or ¯ if it stands for the long sound.

1. camel   *căm/el*
2. acorn   ā/corn
3. palace   păl/ace
4. damage   dăm/age
5. paper   pā/per
6. closet   clŏs/et
7. famous   fā/mous
8. medal   mĕd/al
9. bacon   bā/con
10. minus   mī/nus

Read the list of words and the sentences. Divide each list word into syllables by drawing a line between the syllables. Then write the word from the list that makes sense in each sentence.

h u/m a n
s e c/o n d
s h a d/o w
f l a/v o r
h a b/i t
p o/n y
p i/l o t
s h i v/e r
m e t/a l
h o/t e l

1. I learned how to ride a *pony* when I was young.
2. Greg won second prize in the art contest.
3. Our room in the hotel is big enough for the whole family.
4. The pilot can fly the airplane at night.
5. Choose the flavor of ice cream you like best.
6. The shed is made of wood and metal.
7. Packing an apple in my lunch is a habit for me.
8. Each February we wait to see if the groundhog will see its shadow.

REVIEW   Syllables

Name

Read the words below. Write each word and draw a line between its syllables.

1. chapter   *chap/ter*
2. undress   un/dress
3. cozy   co/zy
4. squeaky   squeak/y
5. magic   mag/ic
6. hopeless   hope/less
7. firewood   fire/wood
8. model   mod/el
9. picnic   pic/nic
10. truthful   truth/ful
11. button   but/ton
12. oatmeal   oat/meal
13. closet   clos/et
14. pretest   pre/test
15. never   nev/er
16. minus   mi/nus
17. doorbell   door/bell
18. notice   no/tice
19. painless   pain/less
20. distrust   dis/trust
21. lemon   lem/on
22. sunny   sun/ny
23. highway   high/way
24. later   la/ter
25. harbor   har/bor
26. wishbone   wish/bone
27. reuse   re/use
28. salad   sal/ad
29. acorn   a/corn
30. slowly   slow/ly
31. unsafe   un/safe
32. rewrite   re/write

Read the words below. Write each word and draw a line between its syllables.

1. refill — *re/fill*
2. friendly — friend/ly
3. yellow — yel/low
4. human — hu/man
5. untie — un/tie
6. displease — dis/please
7. pencil — pen/cil
8. notebook — note/book
9. petal — pet/al
10. cheerful — cheer/ful

Read the list of words and the sentences. Divide each list word into syllables by drawing a line between the syllables. Then write the word from the list that makes sense in each sentence.

tra/vel
cloud/y
star/fish
bed/room
fa/mous
neat/ly
mis/take
un/load
doc/tor
fin/ish

1. I visit the *doctor* at least once a year.
2. The team will __travel__ to the city next weekend.
3. A __famous__ singer will sing in this show.
4. I made only one __mistake__ on my math test.
5. The __cloudy__ sky made us afraid that we wouldn't be able to have our picnic.
6. When I __finish__ my homework, I can watch the television show.
7. There are two beds in my __bedroom__.
8. Please help us __unload__ the boxes from the truck.

Safety Rules

Read the following important rules for street safety. Follow these rules yourself and help others follow them, too.

1. Cross streets only at the corners.
2. Always look both ways before you cross the street.
3. Do not cross the street when the light is red. Wait until the light turns to green.
4. Do not walk between parked cars.
5. Always walk on the left side of the road, facing the cars.
6. Stop, look, and listen before you cross the railroad tracks. Be sure no train is coming.
7. Do not ride your bicycle on the sidewalk.
8. Help little children cross the street safely.
9. Do not get into a car with a stranger.
10. Find a police officer when you see trouble.

A. Finish each rule with the right word or words.

1. Cross only at __corners__.
2. __Stop__, __look__, and __listen__ before you cross the railroad tracks.
3. Never get into a car with a __stranger__.
4. Don't ride your bicycle on the __sidewalk__.
5. Walk on the __left__ side of the road, __facing__ the cars.
6. When you see trouble, you should find a __police officer__.
7. Before you cross the street, you should look __both__ ways.

B. Finish each idea in your own words. *Answers may vary. Suggested answers are given.*

1. A police officer is someone who __can help you__
2. A stranger is someone __you don't know__
3. A red light means __stop__
4. A green light means __go__

C. Think about these questions. Write answers for two of them.
   Why should you walk on the left side of the road, facing the cars?
   Why shouldn't you walk between parked cars?
   Why should you stop, look, and listen before you cross the railroad tracks?
   Why shouldn't you ride your bicycle on the sidewalk?

Answers will vary but might include the following ideas.

1. You should walk on the left side of the road, facing the cars, so you can see what's coming on your side of the road.

   You shouldn't walk between parked cars because drivers might not be able to see you.

2. You should stop, look, and listen before you cross the railroad tracks to be sure no train is coming.

   You shouldn't ride your bicycle on the sidewalk because you might injure other people.

Antonyms

Words to use: light–heavy, everything–nothing, loose–tight, cool–warm, true–untrue, fat–thin, bright–dull, tame–wild, large–tiny, full–empty, noisy–quiet

Name

An antonym is a word that has the opposite meaning of another word.

early – late

Read the words in each box below. Draw a line to match each word with its antonym (opposite).

large — old
young — weak
strong — small

few — many
off — after
before — on

slow — hot
cold — fast
over — under

save — bumpy
smooth — spend
early — late

always — fair
unfair — dry
wet — never

day — night
yes — no
frown — smile

Read the list of words below. Then read the sentences that follow. Write the word from the list that is an antonym (opposite) for the underlined word in each sentence.

light   unkind   shut   shout
false   to   down   awake

1. This letter is <u>from</u> Uncle Todd. — *to*
2. I was <u>asleep</u> when Grandfather called. — awake
3. Is this living room always so <u>dark</u>? — light
4. Please help me <u>open</u> this heavy door. — shut
5. I will <u>whisper</u> the clue to you. — shout
6. Is the answer to this question <u>true</u>? — false
7. Please walk <u>up</u> the steps with me. — down
8. Writing that letter was <u>kind</u>. — unkind

Synonyms

Name _____

A synonym is a word that has the same or nearly the same meaning as another word.

gift – present

Read the words in each box below. Draw a line to match each word with its synonym (word that has the same meaning).

talk – speak
unhappy – sad
small – little

hurt – harm
gift – present
fast – quick

listen – hear
rush – hurry
nice – kind

glad – happy
forest – woods
trail – path

big – large
say – tell
pretty – beautiful

clean – wash
breeze – wind
shout – yell

Read the list of words below. Then read the sentences that follow. Write the word from the list that is a synonym (word that has the same meaning) for the underlined word in each sentence.

nice   cool   run   noisy
crowd   strength   sofa   soil

1. Carmen and Jimmy are sitting on the <u>couch</u>.　　*sofa*
2. There was a <u>mob</u> of people in the store.　　crowd
3. Because it is <u>chilly</u> outside, I will wear a sweater.　　cool
4. Does Kenny have the <u>power</u> to lift that load?　　strength
5. Would your uncle like to <u>jog</u> with us?　　run
6. It was <u>kind</u> of Carly to show me this book.　　nice
7. I woke up when I heard the <u>loud</u> horn.　　noisy
8. Do you have enough <u>dirt</u> for that plant?　　soil

Antonyms and Synonyms

Name _____

Read the words below. Circle the two words in each row that are antonyms (opposites).

1. shiny　(large)　(small)　red　round
2. fair　(happy)　little　(sad)　new
3. (cooked)　yes　save　(raw)　slow
4. nice　hot　tall　(rich)　(poor)
5. cost　(sink)　send　(float)　grow
6. mix　play　(sold)　sweet　(bought)

Read each sentence and the words beside it. Complete each sentence by writing the word that is a synonym (word that has the same meaning) for the word shown below the blank.

1. I will try not to *harm* the plants when I walk through the garden. (hurt)　　harm / water
2. My *friends* and I like to eat lunch together. (pals)　　aunt / friends
3. This map shows where my *road* is. (street)　　road / home
4. I knew she was happy by the *smile* on her face. (grin)　　smile / look
5. I made a *gift* for Timmy's birthday. (present)　　cake / gift
6. Does Carl know how to *repair* a flat tire? (fix)　　remove / repair

---

REVIEW   Antonyms and Synonyms

Name _____

Read each pair of sentences. In the blanks, write a pair of antonyms (opposites) from the sentences.

1. My father sold his old car last week.　　*sold*
   I bought some paper for my art class.　　*bought*
2. My basket is full of shiny red apples.　　full
   The empty shoe boxes are on the steps.　　empty
3. We will be riding over a bumpy road.　　bumpy
   The lake looks smooth this morning.　　smooth
4. Whisper the clue to your partner.　　Whisper
   I heard you shout my name.　　shout

Read each pair of sentences. In the blanks, write a pair of synonyms (words that have the same meaning) from the sentences.

1. What kind of present should I make for him?　　*present*
   I saved my money to buy her a birthday gift.　　*gift*
2. The school is near the city park.　　near
   Does your aunt live close to my friend's home?　　close
3. The teacher read the story to the class.　　story
   Would you like to hear a tale about a rabbit?　　tale
4. If we hurry to the school, we can see the show.　　hurry
   Because we were running out of time, we had to rush.　　rush

---

PROGRESS CHECK   Antonyms and Synonyms

Name _____

Read the list of words below. Then read the sentences that follow. Write the word from the list that is an antonym (opposite) for the underlined word in each sentence.

never   float   late
strong   save   bought

1. I would like to <u>spend</u> some money this year.　　*save*
2. Am I here too <u>early</u> to see the show?　　late
3. Jake <u>always</u> brings his lunch from home.　　never
4. The toy boat will <u>sink</u> when you put it in the water.　　float
5. Running races has made my legs feel <u>weak</u>.　　strong
6. I <u>sold</u> baskets of flowers at the market.　　bought

Read the list of words below. Then read the sentences that follow. Write the word from the list that is a synonym (word that has the same meaning) for the underlined word in each sentence.

unhappy   cool   glad
present   path   pretty

1. I felt <u>sad</u> when my friend moved.　　*unhappy*
2. The colored lights of the city look <u>beautiful</u>.　　pretty
3. He made the painting as a <u>gift</u> for his uncle.　　present
4. The wind makes me feel <u>chilly</u>.　　cool
5. I am <u>happy</u> that you could be with us today.　　glad
6. This <u>trail</u> leads to some picnic tables.　　path

Homophones

Name

Words to use: piece-peace, hall-haul, would-wood, soar-sore, sun-sun, blue-blew, beat-beet, ring-wring, in-inn, through-threw, ar-oar

Homophones are words that sound the same but have different spellings and different meanings.

| would - wood |

Read the words. Draw a line to match each word with its homophone (word that sounds the same).

your	tow	night	knight	week	hear
toe	you're	knew	tale	here	sent
wait	weight	tail	new	cent	pale
too	sale	deer	dear	pail	weak
sail	two	maid	made	sea	see

Read each pair of sentences. In the blanks, write a pair of homophones (words that sound the same) from the sentences.

1. The book you want is on the right side of the shelf. — *right*

   Please write a letter to me soon. — *write*

2. My nose always gets sunburned when I'm at the beach. — nose

   Edward knows the way to the new classroom. — knows

3. Where can I buy some fishing line for my new rod? — buy

   We went by the street where you used to live. — by

4. There is a big knot in that jump rope. — knot

   Penny will not be running in the next race. — not

5. Before I bake bread, I must buy some flour. — flour

   The flower will look nice in this tall yellow vase. — flower

---

Homographs

Name

Homographs are words that have the same spelling but different meanings. Sometimes they are pronounced differently.

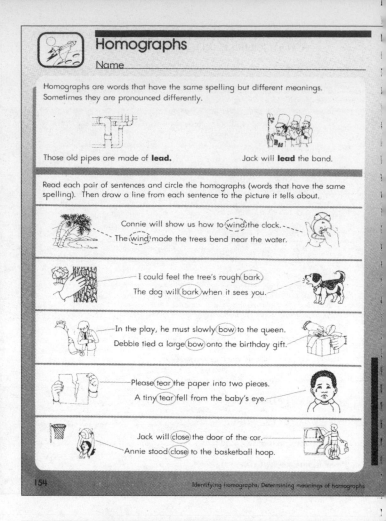

Those old pipes are made of **lead**.

Jack will **lead** the band.

Read each pair of sentences and circle the homographs (words that have the same spelling). Then draw a line from each sentence to the picture it tells about.

- Connie will show us how to (wind) the clock.
- The (wind) made the trees bend near the water.

- I could feel the tree's rough (bark).
- The dog will (bark) when it sees you.

- In the play, he must slowly (bow) to the queen.
- Debbie tied a large (bow) onto the birthday gift.

- Please (tear) the paper into two pieces.
- A tiny (tear) fell from the baby's eye.

- Jack will (close) the door of the car.
- Annie stood (close) to the basketball hoop.

Homophones and Homographs

Name

Read the words below. Circle the two words in each row that are homophones (words that sound the same).

1.	been	(bear)	bake	(bare)	bale
2.	(beat)	beak	bead	(beet)	bean
3.	sink	(cent)	seem	center	(scent)
4.	(I)	I've	(eye)	egg	elf
5.	send	(sea)	(see)	sell	seat
6.	heat	head	he	(heal)	(heel)

Read the homographs (words that have the same spelling) and their meanings below. Then read the sentences that follow. In each sentence, decide the meaning of the underlined homograph. Write the letter of the correct meaning in the blank.

lead	**tear**	**close**
A. a heavy metal	A. to rip	A. to shut
B. to show the way	B. a drop of water from the eye	B. near

1. The pipes in the old building are made of <u>lead</u>. *A*

2. Did I see a <u>tear</u> fall from your eye? B

3. Russell stood <u>close</u> to his sister. B

4. Who will <u>lead</u> us to the lake? B

5. Please <u>close</u> the book when you are done reading the chapter. A

6. Use the edge of the box to <u>tear</u> the wrapping paper. A

Homophones and Homographs

REVIEW

Name

Read each pair of sentences. In the blanks, write a pair of homophones (words that sound the same) from the sentences.

1. I knew you would like to go walking through the city. — *knew*

   The tall building you see on this street is new. — *new*

2. Please meet me at the school lunchroom. — meet

   What kind of meat should I use in the soup? — meat

3. Carry the water in a little pail. — pail

   When I was sick, my face looked pale. — pale

4. You may use this oar in the rowboat. — oar

   Come to my house before or after lunch. — or

5. I will be sailing for eight days. — eight

   The puppy ate all of its food today. — ate

Read the list of homographs (words that have the same spelling) below. Then read each pair of meanings that follows. Write the homograph from the list that matches both meanings.

wind	bark	close	tear	bow	lead

1. A. to bend the head or body   B. a knot made of ribbon — *bow*

2. A. to shut   B. near — close

3. A. moving air   B. to turn or tighten — wind

4. A. water from the eye   B. to rip — tear

Homophones and Homographs

Name

Read each pair of sentences. In the blanks, write a pair of homophones (words that sound the same) from the sentences.

1. The cut will heal quickly if it is kept clean.   _heal_

   My left shoe needs a new heel.   _heel_

2. She knew the answer to the question.   _knew_

   I found the new book on the top of the bookshelf.   _new_

3. I rode to the woods on a brown pony.   _rode_

   Which road leads to the shopping center?   _road_

4. The bear cubs in the zoo are so playful.   _bear_

   I walked in the sand in my bare feet.   _bare_

Read the homographs (words that have the same spelling) and their meanings below. Then read the sentences that follow. In each sentence, decide the meaning of the underlined homograph. Write the letter of the correct meaning in the blank.

wind	**bow**	**tear**
A. moving air	A. to bend the head or body	A. to rip
B. to turn or twist	B. a knot made of ribbon	B. a drop of water from the eye

1. You need to <u>wind</u> the key on that toy to make it work.   _B_

2. Please put a yellow <u>bow</u> on that gift.   _B_

3. How did you <u>tear</u> your shirt?   _A_

4. The <u>wind</u> blew the leaves across the lawn.   _A_

Assessment of identifying homophones; Determining meanings of homographs   157

Alphabetical Order

Name

You can put words in alphabetical order by looking at the first letter of each word. If the first letters of the words are the same, look at the second letters. If the second letters of the words are the same, look at the third letters.

drank
drive
drum

Read the lists of words. Number each list of words in alphabetical order.

List 1		List 2		List 3		List 4	
nail	1	price	5	clean	4	bring	4
nut	6	paint	1	city	3	blink	2
nine	4	pink	2	crown	6	broke	5
next	2	put	6	call	1	black	1
night	3	plum	3	coin	5	bread	3
noise	5	pond	4	cent	2	brush	6

Read the groups of words. Write each group of words in alphabetical order.

cream crumb cry cross crack	hide home heat hall hunt	shelf shine shoe shut sharp
1. _crack_	1. _hall_	1. _sharp_
2. _cream_	2. _heat_	2. _shelf_
3. _cross_	3. _hide_	3. _shine_
4. _crumb_	4. _home_	4. _shoe_
5. _cry_	5. _hunt_	5. _shut_

158   Alphabetizing by second and third letters

Guide Words

Name

The two words at the top of a dictionary page are called guide words. The first guide word is the same as the first word listed on the page. The second guide word is the same as the last word listed on the page. To find a word in the dictionary, decide if it comes in alphabetical order between the guide words on a page. If it does, you will find the word on that page.

Read each pair of guide words and the words that are listed below them. Circle the four words in each list that could be found on a page that has those guide words.

draw / foil	**melt / pony**	**boat / cone**
dime	(past)	crown
(drink)	(open)	(bride)
(face)	match	(cloud)
from	prize	(call)
(dust)	(must)	(chain)
(fire)	(nine)	cut

get / heavy	**rose / stand**	**two / wrote**
(grow)	rich	tractor
(happy)	(slide)	turtle
house	(rush)	(under)
icy	(scarf)	(voice)
(give)	(some)	(world)
(goat)	return	(wind)

Using guide words   159

Guide Words

Name

Read the six pairs of guide words and their dictionary page numbers. Then read the lists of words that follow. Write the page number on which each list word would be found in the dictionary.

apple / bend—p. 6	**both / bunch**—p. 8	**flight / give**—p. 26
glove / happy—p. 28	**roar / send**—p. 46	**sink / use**—p. 48

1. as   _p. 6_
2. smell   _p. 48_
3. gaze   _p. 26_
4. bright   _p. 8_
5. breeze   _p. 8_
6. goat   _p. 28_
7. sand   _p. 46_
8. grown   _p. 28_
9. band   _p. 6_
10. speak   _p. 48_
11. base   _p. 6_
12. those   _p. 48_

13. branch   _p. 8_
14. geese   _p. 26_
15. rust   _p. 46_
16. brown   _p. 8_
17. art   _p. 6_
18. grape   _p. 28_
19. rug   _p. 46_
20. fresh   _p. 26_
21. bark   _p. 6_
22. sold   _p. 48_
23. rule   _p. 46_
24. guess   _p. 28_

160   Using guide words

Read the lists of words below. Then read the guide words that follow. Write each list word below the correct pair of guide words. Then number each list of words to show how they would be listed in alphabetical order.

bench	cane	lunch	change	must
leave	ashes	my	born	city
buy	make	oak	law	barn
noise	nice	answer	chew	lime

Words may be listed in any order.

1. above / broke

bench	4
ashes	2
answer	1
born	5
barn	3

2. butter / corn

buy	1
cane	2
change	3
chew	4
city	5

3. lamb / mice

leave	2
make	5
lunch	4
law	1
lime	3

4. mountain / old

noise	4
nice	3
my	2
oak	5
must	1

Read each pair of guide words and the words that are listed below them. Circle the four words in each list that could be found on a page that has those guide words.

held / ink

hall
(hide)
(ice)
(horse)
(howl)
itself

jeep / leave

(large)
jail
(join)
(judge)
(June)
lift

mist / nine

(monkey)
march
(name)
melt
(myself)
(neat)

seat / such

(shelf)
(south)
(spare)
science
swing
(smoke)

Read the four pairs of guide words and their dictionary page numbers. Then read the lists of words that follow. Write the page number on which each list word would be found in the dictionary.

above / are—p. 1   **arm / blue**—p. 2
both / child—p. 5   **cord / dime**—p. 7

1. ate	p. 2	8. always	p. 1	15. dawn	p. 7
2. add	p. 1	9. bush	p. 5	16. bunk	p. 5
3. cost	p. 7	10. air	p. 1	17. aunt	p. 2
4. brick	p. 5	11. desk	p. 7	18. chest	p. 5
5. awake	p. 2	12. angry	p. 1	19. curl	p. 7
6. being	p. 2	13. apple	p. 1	20. cent	p. 5
7. animal	p. 1	14. base	p. 2	21. creek	p. 7

Read the lists of words below. Then read the guide words that follow. Write each list word below the correct pair of guide words. Then number each list of words to show how they would be listed in alphabetical order.

knee	heat	valley	idea	twelve
high	upon	listen	its	ice
uncle	jam	lace	jelly	job
lead	lump	hope	join	us

Words may be listed in any order.

1. harm / inch

high	2
heat	1
hope	3
idea	5
ice	4

2. is / kept

jam	2
its	1
jelly	3
join	5
job	4

3. kind / mercy

knee	1
lead	3
lump	5
listen	4
lace	2

4. turn / village

uncle	2
upon	3
valley	5
twelve	1
us	4

Weather

Everyone talks about the weather, but no one does anything about it. Have you ever heard this saying? There's not much anyone *can* do about the weather. Would you like to have a picnic or go swimming? Do you want to go ice skating or ride your sled? The weather may decide what you can do.

Hot and Cold

In many places, it is hot in the summer. In the winter, it is cold. In the spring and fall, it may be warm on some days and cool on others. Knowing if it will be hot, warm, cool, or cold can help you decide how to dress and what kind of work or play you can do.

Wind

Air that moves sideways is called wind. A wind that blows from the north is cold, and a wind that blows from the south may be warm. The speed of the wind can change the weather.

Clouds

The clouds in the sky can also change the weather. There are different kinds of clouds. Many people can tell from the kind of clouds in the sky what the weather is going to be like. Some clouds mean rain; other clouds mean fair weather.

1. Check the word that tells the main idea.

_____ picnics   ✓ weather   _____ clouds

2. Check each group of words that tells something that can change the weather.

✓ the speed of the wind

_____ the kind of clothes you wear

✓ the kind of clouds in the sky